CRITICAL PERSPECTIVES ON RURAL CHANGE

Volume 3

RURAL ENTERPRISE

RURAL ENTERPRISE

Shifting Perspectives on Small-Scale Production

Edited by
SARAH WHATMORE,
PHILIP LOWE
AND
TERRY MARSDEN

Routledge
Taylor & Francis Group
LONDON AND NEW YORK

First published in 1991 by David Fulton Publishers Ltd.

This edition first published in 2023
by Routledge
4 Park Square, Milton Park, Abingdon, Oxon OX14 4RN

and by Routledge
605 Third Avenue, New York, NY 10158

Routledge is an imprint of the Taylor & Francis Group, an informa business

British Library Cataloguing in Publication Data
A catalogue record for this book is available from the British Library

ISBN: 978-1-032-49781-5 (Set)
ISBN: 978-1-032-49665-8 (Volume 3) (hbk)
ISBN: 978-1-032-49695-5 (Volume 3) (pbk)
ISBN: 978-1-003-39504-1 (Volume 3) (ebk)

DOI: 10.4324/9781003395041

Publisher's Note
The publisher has gone to great lengths to ensure the quality of this reprint but points out that some imperfections in the original copies may be apparent.

Disclaimer
The publisher has made every effort to trace copyright holders and would welcome correspondence from those they have been unable to trace.

CRITICAL PERSPECTIVES
ON
RURAL CHANGE SERIES

RURAL ENTERPRISE

SHIFTING PERSPECTIVES ON SMALL-SCALE PRODUCTION

EDITED BY

SARAH WHATMORE
PHILIP LOWE
TERRY MARSDEN

David Fulton Publishers
London

David Fulton Publishers Ltd
2 Barbon Close, London WC1N 3JX

First published in Great Britain by
David Fulton Publishers, 1991

Note: The right of the contributors to be identified as the authors of their work has been asserted by them in accordance with the Copyright, Designs and Patents Act 1988.

British Library Cataloguing in Publication Data

Rural enterprise: shifting perspectives on small-scale production.
- (Critical perspectives on rural change v. 3)
1. Agriculture
I. Whatmore, Sarah II. Lowe, Philip III. Marsden, Terry
338.1091734

ISBN 1-85346-113-X

Typeset by Chapterhouse, Formby L37 3PX
Printed and bound in Great Britain by
Biddles Ltd, Guildford and King's Lynn

Contents

Contributors

Susan Boucher	Department of Geography University of Bristol UK
Chris Curtin	Department of Political Science and Sociology University College Galway Ireland
Andrew Flynn	Bartlett School of Architecture and Planning University College London UK
Imre Kovach	Institute for Social Research Budapest Hungary
Philip Lowe	Bartlett School of Architecture and Planning University College London UK
Terry Marsden	Department of Planning, Housing and Development South Bank Polytechnic London UK
Raffaele Paloscia	Institute of Urban and Regional Studies Florence Italy
Colin Sage	Wye College University of London UK

PREFACE

Critical Perspectives on Rural Change Series

This series aims to promote the international dissemination and debate of current empirical and theoretical research relevant to rural areas in advanced societies. Rural areas, their residents and agencies face considerable change and uncertainty. The balance between production, consumption and conservation is being adjusted as economic activities are relocated and primary production is transformed. Similarly the values placed upon rural living and landscapes are altering. Local and external political forces structure choices within rural areas, not only for those concerned with agriculture, but also with regard to rural development, general economic and social policy, and regional fiscal arrangements. To understand contemporary rural change, therefore, demands a critical and holistic perspective able to transcend traditional disciplinary boundaries and to encompass different spatial and institutional levels of analysis. The series is intended to contribute to the development of such a perspective, and the volumes are designed to attract a wide audience associated with international comparative research. Each provides a review of current research within its subject. This, the third volume, focuses on the relationships between rurality and small-scale production. It is intended to explore the diversity and significance of rural small-scale production in different countries and the regional and disciplinary theoretical discourses which inform current research.

Sarah Whatmore
Philip Lowe
Terry Marsden
Bristol 1991

CHAPTER 1

Artisan or Entrepreneur? Refashioning Rural Production

Sarah Whatmore, Philip Lowe and Terry Marsden

Over the last ten years or so, advanced industrial countries and transitional socialist countries alike have rediscovered the social and economic significance of small-scale forms of commercial production including small enterprises, self-employment and 'informal' market activities (Scase, 1989). Almost simultaneously, researchers and policy-makers in these countries have recognised that large numbers of people make a living, and large quantities of economic goods are produced, outside the dominant institutions of the market and the state economy. One of the remarkable aspects of this growing interest in small-scale production is the pervasive sense that something new is being uncovered in terms of both the phenomena under scrutiny and the theoretical efforts to make sense of them; remarkable because of its dissonance with established analytical and political interest in the durability of such forms of production in rural regions, particularly in southern Europe and the so-called third world.

The association between crafts, artisanal activities, self-provisioning and family enterprise, and rural localities runs deep (Long, 1984). Interpretations of one reinforce interpretations of the other. In scientific terms this association informs persistent attempts to explain why such 'traditional' forms of production have never lost their significance in agriculture, despite the processes of capitalist and socialist industrialisation which have characteristically restructured production within more corporate, or collective, and less individualistic forms (Bernstein, 1986). As significant are more popular 'common sense' representations of small-scale production as an historical curiosity preserved by the strength of traditional cultural practices in regions at the margins of processes of modernisation, centred on the industrial city. Such popular and scientific accounts have fired some dramatic social changes in the countryside as they have been taken up and transformed as objects of market exchange or state policy. An extreme example was Romania's notorious 'systematisation of rural settlements' programme to forcibly 'modernise' rural social and economic relations.

The upheavals of modern industrialised society, reflected in a profusion of epoch-marking terms – 'post-fordist', 'post-modern' and 'post-socialist' – have stimulated a new found interest in small-scale production. In the light of these developments, the once deviant social and economic relations of the countryside are being invested with a new significance. What were once seen to be the disadvantages of rural areas and the causes of their marginality are being increasingly reinterpreted as advantages and sources of dynamism. Some commentators have suggested already that rural sociology now has an opportunity to influence a wider community of researchers and policy-makers looking to it to provide tried and tested models of small-scale forms of production (Benvenuti, 1985). Others, particularly in central Europe, go further, reinterpreting the durability of traditional forms of production in rural areas not as a barrier to progress but as having safeguarded the pre-Communist culture and skills of individual enterprise and, hence, as providing the seed-bed for new social movements, political alliances and economic relations (Szelenyi, 1988).

Conjectures of this kind raise important analytical challenges which it is appropriate to address in a series on 'critical perspectives on rural change'. Exposed to the light of diverse regional experiences and research literatures, the nature and significance of rural small-scale production emerge as highly contested and complex issues. The overall theme of this volume is the interweaving of 'rurality' and 'small-scale production' at empirical, theoretical and ideological levels, and contemporary shifts in their configuration and connotation in particular contexts. This theme is addressed in various ways by each of the chapters, guided by three more specific concerns:

(1) to bring together research on small-scale rural enterprise in the parallel, but often poorly related, *theoretical discourses* which characterise work on countries in the so-called first, second and third worlds;
(2) to explore the diversity and significance of contemporary *social and economic forms* of rural small-scale production evident in countries positioned very differently in this global hierarchy;
(3) to consider the complex representational and ideological processes by which small-scale production and rural localities are woven together in state policy under very different *political regimes*.

The geographical focus of this collection is more specifically European than in previous volumes, deliberately so at a moment when these issues have a particular resonance in the shifting terrain of Europe and the intense political struggle over its 'common future'. But, at the same time, we have widened our geographical scope to include work on the 'developing world' which, we believe, has particularly important theoretical contributions to make as well as providing instructive comparative cases. All the chapters contribute in some way to each of the interrelated concerns set out above, but they are organised in terms of their main emphasis on the theoretical, socio-economic, and political dimensions in turn.

Theoretical issues

Clearly the term 'small-scale production' used above does not represent a coherent theoretical category in social or economic terms. It covers businesses below a specified size of workforce or output and 'informal' forms of income generation and production. Pahl (1989), amongst others, rightly cautions against conflating smallness of scale and informality. Here, we are concerned with their interrelationship and manifestation in a variety of social and economic forms which build on, and play a part in constructing, specific rural identities. A characteristic shared by many forms of economic activity which are included under this umbrella term is that they fall outside the organisational forms of the mainstream economy. Attempts to theorise such phenomena thus face a common difficulty in that they are embedded within a conceptual framework mapped out in relation to dominant economic structures and, hence, tend to construct small-scale forms of production in oppositional terms as residual, anomalous or, to borrow a parallel from post-structuralist analysis, as 'the other'. In short, the research process itself has played a part in fashioning the marginality of such forms of production as well as their new found significance.

This oppositional stance can be traced through many social science disciplines, but perhaps the most influential has been that emanating from Economics - the concept of the 'informal' economy defined as a separate sector or realm of economic activity outside, or distinct from, the 'formal' or dominant one. Sharpe identifies two dimensions underlying numerous attempts to define and categorise such activities. One is concerned with the kind of value derived from them ranging between the extremes of work in exchange for wages, in the market or the state workplace, and work producing goods for direct consumption unmediated by the money economy. The second dimension concerns the state regulation of work activities, ranging from work regulated for taxation, welfare and accounting purposes, to work outside state regulation on one or more of these counts (1988). This term has widespread currency in academic and policy circles in industrialised and developing countries (see, for example, Harding and Jenkins, 1989; and Bromley and Gerry, 1979). The term 'second' economy has an equivalent place in the central European research tradition but here, in the circumstances of a much more centralised political apparatus controlling the economy, the primary emphasis has been on the evasion of state regulation.

From a more sociological perspective we can find parallel theoretical categories. In the western political economy tradition efforts have focused on making sense of such phenomena as forms of production, characterised by the 'unity' of property and labour (Redclift and Mingione, 1985). Particularly influential has been the theoretical category of 'petty commodity production' which has spawned a number of derivations, such as 'simple' and 'domestic' commodity production, variably stressing the significance of household and kinship relations to the organisation of these forms of production (see MacEwan Scott, 1986). Associated attempts have been made to position those engaged in such forms of economic activity in terms of social class structures, with the widespread adoption of the label 'petite bourgeoisie'. Here again, such theoretical categories express the anomalous status of these phenomena, characterising them as 'an uneasy stratum' or as occupying a 'contradictory class location' (Bechhofer and Elliott, 1981). More proscriptive theorisations can be found in central European sociological thinking, placing much greater stress on the 'deviancy' of these social categories, as pre-, or even anti-, socialist class relations (Davis, 1989).

In an important paper, Peattie (1987) traces the growing currency of the term 'informal sector' to its political roots in efforts to calculate national accounts, on the one hand, and to assess and tackle poverty and welfare issues on the other, particularly in the 'third world'. She argues forcefully that the well established analytical shortcomings of the term have helped, rather than hindered, its spread and legitimacy precisely because its 'fuzziness' makes it amenable to the political purposes and policy practices of a wide range of governments and quasi-government agencies. She goes on to suggest that while the categories of the political economy tradition have a much better purchase on the theoretical significance of small-scale production, their influence has been severely restricted by the ideological 'taint' of their Marxist origins.

One of the general problems shared in common by these approaches is the way in which they cast the economic and social relations of small-scale forms of production as fixed objects rather than as dynamic processes. Such oppositional categories are part of wider dualistic patterns of thinking which tend to (re)construct these social and economic relations in the shape of definite sectors or spheres, such that the dominant and muted categories of economic activity come to occupy separate analytical spaces. Castells and Portes argue that this problem can only be avoided if we understand 'informal' economic activity as a process, rather than as a thing, whose central feature is that it is unregulated by the institutions of society (1989: 1–12). Pahl goes further (1989), suggesting that rather than focus on informal activities in terms of forms of production or types of economy they are better understood as forms of work, characterised by non-wage relations. This requires an analytical framework that incorporates the *meaning* of the activities being undertaken by those engaged in them in the context of the wider social relations in which they are embedded (p. 106). Moves away from defining separate sectors and identifying their interdependencies have been growing, influenced particularly by feminist arguments and analysis in anthropology and other social sciences which advocate a revision of the whole conception of political economy, shifting the focus of study from the organisation of production to the organisation of livelihood (Moore, 1988).

In chapter 2 Terry Marsden deals directly with these theoretical difficulties and suggests ways forward in critical rural research centred on contemporary departures from the categorical logic of petty commodity production. He focuses on one of the most notable fields in which these concepts have been applied and developed - agrarian political economy. Here concern has centred on exploring the circumstances of family or household based forms of production in farming in contemporary advanced industrial and developing countries. He highlights some of the major stimuli for recent developments in terms of the analytical problems that researchers in this tradition have encountered and sought to overcome. He argues strongly for a shift of emphasis away from a focus on discrete forms of production towards a concern with the *process* of commoditisation and the ways in which commodity and non-commodity relations are being reworked, generating new and diverse small-scale social forms and economic practices.

The other essays in this volume examine particular aspects of the empirical nature and significance of small-scale rural production in different countries, informed by particular regional and disciplinary theoretical perspectives. One of the major hindrances to the development of more conceptually sophisticated analyses is the relative isolation of these different theoretical discourses such that, as yet, there is remarkably little work which brings the experiences and interpretations of specific contexts together (but see Redclift and Mingione, 1985; Portes *et al.*, 1989). This volume covers the range of concepts brought to bear on small-scale economic activity identified above, including - 'second economy' (chapter 5), 'household livelihood' (chapter 4), 'artisanal production' (chapter 3) 'petit capitalism' (chapter 6) and the 'small business' (chapter 7). In juxtaposition, these later chapters raise important questions about the assumptions which underlie each of these concepts and, in breaching the insularity of the particular circumstances and traditions from which they stem, suggest some areas for further theoretical development.

Social and economic forms

Chapters 3 to 5 shift the focus to look at contemporary social and economic forms of small-scale production in rural areas and their significance in the very different circumstances of countries in southern Europe, Latin America and central Europe. Some of these represent new or emergent forms of production and labour; the chapters on Hungary and Italy, despite their many differences, examine cases which are usually cast in this light. The Bolivian study examines the longer standing case of small-scale forms of brewing, but makes it clear that these cannot be treated as static, relic forms of production. What the authors of all three chapters emphasise is the dynamism of rural small-scale forms of production and labour and their transmutability in different contexts over long historical periods. In so doing they expose the dangers of too easily designating contemporary manifestations of these forms of production as 'new'; as if they were the indigenous creations of externally driven processes of restructuring without specific genealogies.

The social and economic relations examined in these chapters highlight three recurring tensions in the analysis of small-scale production. The first centres on the interpretation of the economic significance of these relations. Contrasting emphasis is placed either on the institutional organisation of the production of commercial goods, with a focus on the 'public' economy of the enterprise, or on the personal organisation of working lives and livelihoods, with a focus on the 'private' economy of the household. A second tension centres on the social significance and class status of those engaged in various forms of small-scale production. Dominant constructions cast them either as an underclass of workers marginalised from, and exploited by, prevailing class interests, or stress the entrepreneurial character and resources of this social stratum and its potential for upward social mobility, or embourgeoisement.

A third tension concerns the specifically rural significance of small-scale forms of production and labour. One set of explanations is couched in terms of the restructuring of global capital and labour relations and, specifically, the increased flexibility in the technological and institutional structure of these relations. From this broadly Marxist perspective, it is argued that these global processes are responsible for creating new spatial divisions of labour in which rural areas have a new-found significance as localities with particularly amenable social relations (Bradley and Lowe, 1984). In a more Weberian vein, explanations are concerned more with the generational transference of particular modes of rationality (Mooney, 1988). Here, emphasis is placed on rural localities as reservoirs of entrepreneurial skills and spirit passed on through family-based, and often land-centred, cultural lineages.

These analytical tensions are articulated differently in different research traditions and resonate unevenly with the circumstances of rural small-scale producers in different politico-economic regimes. They seem to us to be creative tensions, to be explored through the detailed study of the circumstances and *experiences* of small-scale producers in specific rural contexts, rather than in any sense resolved through generalised theoretical principles. The next three chapters represent valuable examples of just such an exploration.

In chapter 3, Raffaele Paloscia re-examines what is, perhaps, the archetypal case associated with the rediscovery of artisanal production – the Terza Italia. He provides an important counter to the somewhat stylised account of the links between artisanal producers and corporate capital promoted by theories of 'flexible specialisation' and a post-Fordist era of industrial organisation (for a critical overview see Gertler, 1988). He traces the rural roots and historical cultural context which created the conditions now fostering the integration of small-scale artisan production into the corporate global economy. In particular his analysis draws attention to the neglected significance of the distinctive agrarian organisation of Tuscany in providing the basis of a unique territorial formation centred on a tradition of artisanship in the countryside with close economic and infrastructural ties to the cities of the region.

Colin Sage provides an important analytical contrast in chapter 4, drawing on theories and perspectives on household production most fully developed in relation to the 'third' world. He uses the household production of beer (*chicha*) in a fairly remote region of rural Bolivia to demonstrate the wider significance of the diversity of cultural and economic roles played by this production process in the local economy and, what he terms, the 'repertoire' of livelihood activities of rural households in many developing countries. He focuses on the central role of gender relations and women's work in the structure and reproduction of such artisanal forms of production, both as livelihood and commodity. His analysis draws on, and outlines, theoretical perspectives on the internal structuring of small-scale/household based production strongly influenced by feminist scholarship which have, thus far, had less impact on European research (see Redclift and Whatmore, 1990).

In chapter 5 Imre Kovach examines the re-emergence of small-scale enterprise in rural Hungary, using the concept of the second economy and stressing its significance for household livelihoods and gross domestic product in a centrally planned context despite, until recently, being officially discouraged. His detailed analysis covers agricultural, industrial and service sectors of production and a diverse range of forms of small-scale economic activity. One of the most important developments in the 1980s was the limited liberalisation of forms of property and work sanctioned by the state, which has encouraged activities in the second economy, including what Kovach terms 'working pools'. These pools represent formalised arrangements between management and workers in state firms to allow groups of workers to use the firm's plant outside official work hours and to distribute the income from the sale of this produce between pool members (see also Stark, 1985). He stresses the importance of such forms of small-scale production in rural areas not only in supplementing sometimes dramatically low living standards but also in realising better work relations and higher quality products.

The political significance of these social and economic forms of production and labour is tangible from each of these analyses in their very different treatments of the relationship between the individual, the family/household and the state. Kovach is the most explicit in his treatment, speculating on the future role of rural small-scale producers in the newly democratised political system in Hungary. But these political themes are taken up and explored more directly in the last two chapters in the volume.

Politics, policies and the state

Small-scale and informal economic activities and their practitioners have gained growing political, as well as social and economic, significance in recent years, entering the public discourse of governments and social movements within very different political contexts. In the tumultuous political climate in eastern Europe, for example, they have rapidly become symbols of popular resistance to post-war regimes and the re-emergence of a long repressed 'entrepreneurial spirit'. In parts of western Europe, industrial recession and widespread state deregulation in the 1980s have seen governments and pressure groups on the political right make much of the virtues of individual enterprise both as a substitute for state responsibilities for social welfare and as a pro-active element in the economy manifested in the shape of 'small businesses' (Weiss, 1988).

The political significance and policy status of small-scale production is highly volatile, articulated in different ways in the populist rhetoric of Left and Right within a wide range of macro-political contexts. Mingione makes a useful analytical distinction about the political significance attached to different social forms of small-scale and informal economic activity between those which do not run counter to the regulatory regime associated with the dominant mode of production and those which primarily challenge the regulatory system (1988: 570). This can be illustrated even within the same nation state. For example, recent British government rhetoric and policy has consistently sought to sustain a precarious distinction between 'good' and 'bad' forms of individual enterprise. Those deemed to evade or undermine state regulation are pejoratively labelled the 'black economy' and singled out for closer policing; those which conform to the regulatory regime, such as self-employment and family businesses, are lauded as standard bearers of the 'enterprise economy' to be liberated from 'red tape' (Keat and Abercrombie, 1990).

Arguably, however, a new convergence in the populist construction of small-scale production can be detected as the political and economic order in Europe is reforged. This convergence centres on a pervasive free market ideology which binds political democratisation to economic liberalisation; personal, to market, freedom. At the very least there are important parallels between the rising political status of small-scale producers, or the *petite bourgeoisie*, in the enterprise culture promoted during the Thatcher years in Britain (Elliott *et al.*, 1988) and their characterisation by commentators on central Europe as a new class of 'socialist entrepreneurs', representing 'the ultimate and real source of countervailing popular power' (Szelenyi, 1988: 8). In both cases, these social strata are being re-invested with a moral significance in normative ideas of social and economic order; an order which has the family at its heart. Here again, a distinctively rural inflection can be traced in the populist rhetoric surrounding small-scale production.

The association between rural small-scale producers (agrarian and non-agrarian) and populist political movements is not new. For example, the small-scale producers have formed the core of populist movements at both extremes of the political spectrum in the nineteenth and early twentieth centuries in Europe and in developing countries in more recent history (Moore, 1969). The elevation of small-scale producers in contemporary populist rhetoric evokes the amplified significance of the family to the structure of rural production as well as consumption particularly as articulated through access to, and ownership of, land as a basic resource.

This has generated a new political significance for rural areas as a territorial base for the development of new social movements championing entrepreneurial values and interests. This interweaving of rural and familial ideologies is long standing and is reflected not just in the politics of rural society but in the wider cultural politics of the symbolic significance of rurality in which small-scale, family based artisanal production merges into the landscape, becoming part of the object preserved and consumed as 'heritage' by society at large.

In different ways the final two chapters in the book are concerned with the political ideologies surrounding rural small-scale production, focusing on the discrepancies between the populist rhetoric and policy practices of a variety of state agencies. In chapter 6 Chris Curtin and Tony Varley look at these discrepancies in Ireland, which has long placed petit capitalist production at the centre of rural development policies, relating the particular circumstances of the Irish case to more general theories of rural populism. Their analysis covers the policy fields of agriculture, manufacturing and 'community enterprise' and emphasises the constraints and contradictions at the heart of populist policies which seek to deliver to an important political constituency against the overriding pressures of international economic relations and corporate institutions over which national governments and agencies have little effective control.

In chapter 7 Susan Boucher, Andrew Flynn and Philip Lowe examine the rural dimensions of Britain's 'enterprise culture'. They argue that rural areas have been promoted as zones of economic potential in an unprecedented way during the 1980s, tracing this to the ideological appeal of rural small-scale producers to 'new right' thinking which has dominated government policy-making circles over this period. Using economic development policy in the county of Devon as a case study, they focus on the contested interpretation of rural industrialisation amongst various central and local state agencies and the impact of their negotiations on industrial development on the ground. Their analysis focuses on the construction of the 'small firm' as an 'appropriate' type of industrial form for rural areas; a construction which centres on a peculiarly English interpretation of the familial and rural ideologies associated with small-scale production and which plays a key role in the reproduction of a distinctive rural culture and society.

The regional experiences and perspectives assembled in these chapters raise important questions for the interweaving futures of rural areas and small-scale production. Just as the latter has been argued to be gaining a new historical meaning (Castells and Portes, 1989), so we have suggested that rurality is being refashioned in its political, economic and social significance through its association with such forms of production. The very different regional and local circumstances and meaning of rural small-scale production brought together in this volume have implications for the mode and purpose of theorising rural enterprise. In particular, we hope that it will assist in raising questions about conventional analytical categories, identifying issues for collaborative exploration and stimulating much needed comparative research and theoretical development in this field.

References

Bechhofer, F. and Elliott, B. (eds) (1981) *The Petite Bourgeoisie. Comparative studies of the uneasy stratum*. London, Macmillan.

Benvenuti, B. (1985) On the dualism between sociology and rural sociology: some hints for the case of modernisation, *Sociologia Ruralis*, xxv: 214–30.

Bernstein, H. (1986) Capitalism and petty commodity production, *Social Analysis*, 8/1: 11–28.

Bradley, T. and Lowe, P. (eds) (1984) *Locality and Rurality*, Norwich, Geobooks.

Bromley, R. and Gerry, C. (eds) (1979) *Casual work and poverty in Third World Cities*. New York, John Wiley and Sons.

Castells, M. and Portes, A. (1989) World underneath: the origins, dynamics and effects of the informal economy, in Portes *et al.* (eds) *The Informal Economy*: 11–40.

Davis, H. (1989) Crisis and conflict in East European state socialism, in Scace, R. (ed) *Industrial Societies*: 193–215.

Elliott, B., McCrone, T. and Bechhofer, F. (1988) Anxieties and ambitions: the petty bourgeoisie and the new right in Britain, in Rose, D. (ed) *Social Structure and Economic Change*: 263–78.

Gershuny, J. (1979) The informal economy: its role in industrial society, *Futures*, 11/1: 3–15.

Gertler, M. (1988) The limits of flexibility: comments on the post-Fordist vision of production and its geography, *Transactions of the Institute of British Geographers*, 13/4: 419–32.

Harding P. and Jenkins, R. (1989) *The myth of the Hidden Economy: Towards a new understanding of informal economic activities*. Milton Keynes, Open University Press.

Keat, R. and Abercrombie, N. (eds) (1990) *Enterprise Culture*. London, Routledge.

Long, N. (ed) (1984) *Family and work in rural societies: perspectives on non-wage labour*. London, Tavistock Publications.

Macewan Scott, A. (1986) Towards a rethinking of petty commodity production, *Social Analysis*, 20: 93–105.

Mingione, E. (1988) Work and informal activities in urban southern Italy, in Pahl, R. (ed) *On work. Historial, comparative and theoretical approaches*: 548–78. Oxford, Blackwell.

Mooney, P. (1988) *My own Boss. Class, rationality and the family farm*. New Jersey, Westview Press.

Moore, B. (1969) *Social origins of dictatorship and democracy*. USA, Duke University Press.

Moore, H. (1988) *Feminism and Anthropology*. Cambridge, Polity Press.

Pahl, R. (1989) From informal economy to forms of work, in Scase, R. (ed) *Industrial Societies*. London, Unwin Hyman.

Peattie, L. (1987) An idea in good currency and how it grew: the informal sector, *World Development*, 15/7: 851–60.

Portes, A., Castells, M. and Benton, L. (eds) (1989) *The Informal Economy. Studies in advanced and less developed countries*. Baltimore, Johns Hopkins University Press.

Redclift, N. (1985) The contested domain: gender, accumulation and the labour process, in Redclift, N. and Mingione, E. (eds) *Beyond Employment*: 92–126. Oxford, Basil Blackwell.

Redclift, N. and Whatmore, S. (1990) Household, consumption and livelihood: ideologies and issues in rural research, in Marsden, T., Lowe, P. and Whatmore, S. (eds) *Rural Restructuring*: 182–97. London, David Fulton Publishers.

Scase, R. (ed) (1989) *Industrial societies: Crisis and division in Western Capitalism and State Socialism*. London, Unwin Hyman.

Sharpe, B. (1988) Informal work and development in the west, *Progress in Human Geography*, 12: 315–36.

Stark, D. (1985) The micropolitics of the firm and the macropolitics of reform: new forms of workplace bargaining in Hungarian enterprises, in Evans P., Reuschemeyer, D. and Stephens, E. (eds) *States versus Markets in the World System*. London, Sage.

Szelenyi, I. (1988) *Socialist Entrepreneurs. Embourgeoisement in Rural Hungary*. Cambridge, Polity Press.

Weiss, L. (1988) *Creating Capitalism. The state and small business since 1945*. Oxford, Basil Blackwell.

CHAPTER 2

Theoretical Issues in the Continuity of Petty Commodity Production

Terry K. Marsden

Introduction

Undoubtedly, the political and ideological times are favouring the re-emergence of the small scale production unit. Indeed, the flip side of an increasingly globalised and transnational economy seems to embody, both in political rhetoric and ideological verve, the recreation and maintenance of a set of values associated with market liberalisation, entrepreneurialism, flexible specialisation and an emphasis on the removal of the 'barriers' and 'constraints' placed on small producers through traditional collective conceptions of workers rights, trades union power and state welfarism. However economically dominant monopoly capital becomes within certain sectors or regions, the presence of small-scale 'petty' producers, relying mainly on their own resources in terms of labour and skills, seems to be a persistent feature. As the contributions to this volume show, this is particularly relevant in rural areas, where traditionally productive activities have been remarkably resistant to the transformatory forces of monopoly industrial capital. In agriculture in particular, the continuity of family based small-scale production has perplexed many social theorists. It has proved a fertile and instructive ground for theoretical debate and, at different periods, has been given high priority on political agenda in both democratic and totalitarian societies. As it became increasingly obvious during the twentieth century that the development of industrial capitalism was failing to destroy 'the awkward class' of family-based producers, national governments were forced into varying degrees of political and economic *compromise* with them. Indeed, treatment of what was seen as the small-scale agrarian sector became a significant way of defining the roles and activities of the late twentieth-century nation-state. We are now witnessing cases, in Eastern Europe for instance, where small-scale peasant/family production is again being seen as central to the post-Stalinist order. Of course, it is not simply the characteristics of 'smallness' which are held out as a virtue; it is a set of socially and ideologically constructed notions associated with private property ownership, family labour employment, and patriarchal relations. Traditional North American notions of rural populism are re-emerging in a more diverse and varied form in other parts of the world. This does not deny the increasing power of multinational capital but, as it will be argued, it tends to legitimise it.

The point must be that, throughout advanced capitalist countries at least, the increasing political and ideological support for encouraging and maintaining small-scale production systems can only be fully understood in *relation to* the general trajectory of large scale, increasingly multinational capital. Rather than see these modes of production as theoretically opposed, or indeed, contradictory, it is necessary to increasingly *link them together*. The first part of this chapter outlines, in some detail, the origins and interpretations of petty commodity production in agriculture. It then provides an assessment of current debates and defines areas for development. These concern the incorporation of the commoditisation debate; subsumption processes; and, third, a consideration of the process of uneven development in comparative perspective. Empirical reference will be made to studies undertaken in Britain.

The theoretical problem

The process of agricultural production in advanced capitalist societies is still largely undertaken by farm families. Whilst they may employ some hired labour they are largely controlled by patriarchal families. For instance, even in the UK, with its relatively high levels of concentration of the farm sector vis-à-vis the rest of Europe, the farm family has increased its proportion of farm labour input largely through adopting new technologies, whilst it has remained doggedly attached to the ownership and control of farmland. The number of farms employing only family types of labour increased from 65 per cent in 1971 to 71 per cent in 1983. Ninety-four per cent of agricultural holdings are run by individual proprietors, partnerships of private (normally family) companies, and no fewer than 97.5 per cent of all English farms are regarded as 'family businesses' in the sense that all business principals, if more than one, are closely related by blood and marriage. For Galeski and Wilkening (1987) for instance:

> Food production has continued to be a family enterprise in most countries of the world, even with increased industrialisation and urbanisation. The family owned and operated enterprise has provided the incentives and the commitment of people to produce for their own needs and for others under a wide range of natural, economic and

> political conditions. The family farm also provides the basis for self sustaining family and community life, as well as a way of producing for the market (p. 1).

The often state-supported but, nevertheless, capitalistic 'market' to which the legions of family producers have been tied, of course, has been far from a benign or static entity. As Cochrane (1979) eloquently outlined, the operation of the agricultural 'treadmill' under conditions of inelastic demand for food, and technological developments in the food sector more generally, have combined to force the less economically efficient family farmers out of business. Historically and sociologically this has not been a straightforward process amongst petty commodity producers, because of their internal abilities to withstand the rigours and economic rationalities of the market for longer than their capitalistic counterparts, who are much more dependent upon hired labour. For instance, the decline of capitalist (wage labour) farms in Prussian Germany and Victorian England was, according to Friedmann (1982), directly a result of competition from family producers in North America. Family based farms in the newly created frontier wheatlands were able to absorb unforeseen market instabilities, whilst the capitalist farms in Europe were dependent on wage labour and held no such ability to adjust. Indeed, because family farms held no responsibility for hired labour, new methods of production could be more readily adopted, helping to even out the disparities between production time and the human labour needed for it.

Nevertheless, as postwar Europe and North America demonstrate, the progressive reduction of family based farms becomes all too real. The twin processes of concentration and centralisation of production, while not necessarily occurring at a rate originally intended by some policy-makers (e.g. the 1968 Mansholt Plan) has been a significant characteristic, reducing the number of family based enterprises, and for some, reducing the salience of an 'agrarian question' (Bonnano, 1990). In terms of levels of farm output and the amount of land occupied, family based holdings can be seen to be playing a decreasing role. In the UK, for instance, by 1975, capitalist farms employing four or more workers contributed over 50 per cent of the total standard man days, and occupied over 50 per cent of total agricultural area, whilst representing only 16 per cent of all holdings. In the US the debates in the mid-1980s concerning the 'disappearing middle' and the resulting increasing 'dualism' in agrarian structures also represented what seemed to be the progressive decrease in the family based farm, however socially resilient its members were seen to be (see Munton and Marsden, 1990).

The dialectics which exist between the seeming resilience of family based forms of production on the one hand and their eventual demise and absorption into monopoly capitalism on the other have provided a rich basis for theoretical debate over the last fifteen years. Whilst some have found this somewhat circular and obtuse, it is worth outlining its key features, given that in empirical reality, both the persistence *and* the transformation of petty commodity producers have validity sociologically and politically. As social agents, petty commodity producers have been capable of influencing the state and policy makers in protecting their rights and conditions of existence. Alternatively, the significant power of industrial capital in the food system can engender proletarianisation and the progressive removal of small family producers.

Two major perspectives can be distinguished concerning petty commodity producers within capitalist social formation. One gives rise to 'transitional' models in which they are viewed as a category of family based producers with strong ethics of self-sufficiency, but also sell part of their produce to pay rents, rates and taxes. Most of the classical theorists (Marx, Weber, Lenin) argued that the lure of market production would mean the eventual demise of most small producers, leading to proletarianisation.

In contrast, 'survival' models (Chayanov, 1925) argue that non-wage labour production is able to prosper *within* a capitalist system, either because it is protected as a cheap source of labour or owing to its social capacities for self-exploitation and reproduction. The maintenance of so many petty commodity producers for so long has tended to raise serious questions over the validity of the 'transitional' model. Friedmann (1986a), in particular, has attempted to construct a revised theoretical model around the survivalist assumptions. For her, the hiring or sale of wage labour by petty commodity producers does not transform them into either capitalists or proletarians. A market in labour is a condition of their existence over the generational cycle, with temporarily surplus children being employed by families temporarily short of labour. Despite the growth of market relations, she argues that

> . . . the law of value stops at the boundaries of the simple commodity enterprise, where internal relations are governed by other principles, generally notions of the gender division of labour, kinship obligations and patriarchy (p. 28).

Friedmann's formulation attempts to weld together some of the notions associated with market domination and Chayanov's emphasis upon the internal social characteristics of petty commodity producers. Family production holds two distinct aspects relating to the relations *in* and *of* production. The relations of production entail a 'contradictory unity' of private property and labour. Family producers, by and large (and indeed increasingly in many capitalist countries), remain *owners* of property despite heavy involvement in the labour needs of the farm; yet unlike 'capitalist' enterprises they are forced into commodity production. As with capitalist enterprises *per se* they must therefore be understood as commodity production; but unlike capitalist production relations they are based on a 'simple' (i.e. family owner based) organisation. At least as important in distinguishing petty commodity production are the relations *in* production. Here it is assumed that kinship and patriarchy prevail and

> . . . the division of labour, patterns of domination and struggle are all shaped by gender and generation (1986b, p. 187).

If, Friedmann argues, there is such a thing as a uniquely 'rural labour process', it lies not only in land, but also in the tensions between family relations internal to the farm itself and the particular commodity relations which impinge upon the farm. She argues:

> The structure of simple commodity production within (and necessarily within) capitalism produces contradictory interests in itself. It combines in one person or family group the contradictory interests of the two predominant classes of capitalism (1986b, p. 188).

Moreover, capital accumulation, whilst it may exist, is secondary to 'the product of family labour'. Where surplus value is abstracted from the labour process it is not established as a real quantity - a distinguishing feature of value relations. However, the ideal form of petty commodity production is inevitably contradictory, first between value and family and second between property and labour.

Friedmann's conceptual constructions have done much to identify the contradictory nature of petty commodity production, and its distinctiveness and continuity in capitalism. In the peasant studies literature it has initiated considerable debate concerning the social conditions of underdevelopment and the resistance to commodity relations (Scott, 1986). Within the agrarian political economy of advanced societies, Friedmann's propositions reopened many long-standing debates concerning the persistence of family farm production in the face of increasing concentration and centralisation of capital (see Goodman and Redclift, 1986; Newby, 1987). Two major concerns have been, first, the degree of distinctiveness of petty commodity production in agriculture; and, second, the reasons for its maintenance. These two issues are worth considering here.

Following Kautsky's original conceptions concerning the distinctiveness of capitalist development in agriculture, (see Banaji, 1977; Hussain and Tribe, 1983), several writers (see Goodman *et al.*, 1987; Mann, 1990) have stressed the point that petty commodity production exists largely *because of* industrial capital's inability to cope with the natural constraints involved in the agricultural production process. Rather than emphasising the significance and strength of the *internal* logic of petty commodity producers in the process of reproduction, they argue that the seasonal nature of the agricultural labour process is such that production time (i.e. the time when capital is employed in commodity production) is greatly in excess of labour time (i.e. the position of the production time during which labour is allocated to creating value). Because of the inability, even with high levels of technology, to eliminate this gap, the land-based production stage remains unattractive to industrial capital. Hence petty commodity producers can remain in real terms. Davis (1980), on the other hand, argues that the persistence of petty commodity producers arises because of the fact that it can be positively advantageous to capital in the long run, with industrial capital exploiting the family labour farmer but leaving risky and uneven investment in land and working capital in the hands of the farm family. Taking this viewpoint one can argue that petty commodity producers - as with the eighteenth century 'putting out' system - can perform many roles and points for investment including self-exploitation of the family members, organising labour, and absorbing redundant urban labour. In this sense one could agree with Friedmann in arguing that petty commodity production is a central, if distinctive, feature of modern capitalism. However, its conditions for existence are not only internally determined. They are structured and restructured around the needs of industrial and financial capital whose interests lie in maintaining a set of dependent linkages 'at arm's length'.

Such interpretations have done much to induce a type of 'peaceful coexistence' between opposing schools of thought over recent years (see Mann and Dickenson, 1980; Mooney, 1986; Mann, 1990). Those who are attached to the 'transitional' or 'transformational' school tend still to view the family labour farm as a residual category in the evolutionary development of agriculture, or at best see petty commodity production as containing 'obstacles' which delay such processes. Alternatively, the more 'survivalist' interpretations tend to stress the internal resilience of petty commodity production whatever the particular forms monopoly capitalism adopts. Interestingly, however, it is important to recognise that there are some important similarities in such theoretical dualities. In the tradition of the nineteenth-century theorists, many writers, on both sides, tend to assume that petty commodity production is an anomaly – a case of what Newby (1987) calls 'arrested marginalisation' – whose existence in empirical reality needs to be *explained away*. In addition, up until recently, as we shall see below, much of the conceptual development fails to examine fully the processes of *transformation* beyond assumptions concerning the demise of petty commodity production. Emphasis instead is placed on the superimposition of the wage relation over and above non-wage family relations. Yet, as it will be argued here, in modern agrarian societies the nature, intensity and quality of such relations is highly diverse both within and between simple commodity producers. Imposing such an internal consistency upon simple commodity production as a theoretically derived 'ideal type' has tended to hide more than it reveals about the true nature of the productive form. For instance, as Bernstein (1986a) points out, reproduction of petty commodity production cannot, particularly in advanced societies, be seen 'simply' as a family based and bounded set of activities. Indeed it is far from bound. It has to confront and incorporate a variety of commodity based relations and petty accumulation strategies within the family household. The need is that particular *interactions* between family organisation, market and production relations should become a focus of attention rather than that any relationship of separation or domination should be assumed between them.

Such observations and criticisms of existing patterns of enquiry and conceptionalisation do little to reduce the necessity to understand more fully the position of petty commodity production in modern agrarian society. They do point to the need to provide a more accommodating and flexible interpretation which attempts to integrate traditional strands of social theory and relate these more centrally and broadly to rural change. This requires a stronger emphasis upon the understanding of process rather than form of production, and it is to a discussion of such processes that we now turn.

Broadening the agenda: the commoditisation debate

Rather than focusing specifically on forms of production, attempts have recently been made to understand the causes and the consequences of the 'capital penetration process' in agrarian structures of advanced societies. Whilst this is by no means an original topic of concern, new issues are being raised and assembled in what can be generally called 'the commoditisation debate'. This concerns the ways in which capital and commodity relations adapt and transform social institutions, most notably farm 'families' and labour as well as social reproduction processes more generally. This approach represents very much a reaction to the earlier theoretical dualities. While not ignoring the centrality of petty commodity production as an integral part of the wider capitalist social formation it is argued that attention should be more directly focused on the dynamic interaction of commodity relations and market mechanisms and how these 'shape and reproduce these specific forms of production' (Long *et al.*, 1986 p. 2).

By the late 1980s increased criticism developed of the earlier and innovative theoretical formulations associated with the persistence of petty commodity production and the process of subsumption of farm production relations by capitalism in advanced economies (see Marsden *et al.*, 1986, 1987; Chevalier, 1983; Long *et al.*, 1986; Whatmore *et al.*, 1987; Scott, 1986). For instance, many of the debates surrounding the existence of petty commodity production suffered because of a failure to elicit a consistent theoretical and methodological framework amongst its proponents. The concentration upon form of production as opposed to the continual process of transformation and the difficulties in relating ideal theoretical constructs to their empirical realities have been recurrent obstacles to progress.

Such criticisms cannot be divorced from a number of deeper problems that relate to the nature of explanation in structural Marxism (Benton, 1984). For instance there was a general assumption that all forms of PCP *must* be explained by reference to a general invariant law or model rather than a series of historically specific or conjectural ones (see Goodman and Redclift, 1986). A further dilemma lay in the primacy given to general economic laws whilst rendering the political and ideological as secondary. Hence, whilst Friedmann (1986) has more recently promoted the significance of the internal *social* processes of family farms as crucial in understanding their reproduction, the economistic framework within which the ideal type of simple commodity production is constructed provides obstacles in exploring these very issues and in assessing their variability. Another constraint has been the inability of structural Marxist approaches to cope with the differentiation of agricultural production relations through an understanding of the uneven development process over time and space (Marsden *et al.*, 1990b; Billings and Tickamyer, 1990). Emphasis has been placed on the identification of unilinear tendencies without sufficiently considering variability in the origins and direction of different types of capitalist development. This has restrained the development of a comparative analysis of petty commodity production in advanced economies (see Buttel, 1982; Marsden *et al.*, 1990b). The process of uneven development is an essential prerequisite to the maintenance of capitalism. It incorporates the opposing tendencies of differentiation of capital penetration and the eventual equalisation of the conditions of production. Petty commodity production is an essential mechanism through which such uneven development is transmitted. In addition, there has been much terminological and conceptual confusion as to what constitutes the precise nature of simple or petty commodity production, or, for that matter, what the effective scales are with which to assess its role in uneven development.

One possible solution to some of these problems requires the construction of separate but interlinked levels of analysis. Alison Scott (1986), for instance, has identified different levels with which to examine petty commodity production. Firstly, **the primary level** of simple commodity production can be identified where the basic conditions for existence at the abstract level are (i) the existence of a market for commodities, (ii) private ownership of the means of production and access to labour outside the wage labour market. At the **secondary level** the linkages are stressed between productive forms and institutions such as the state. Here *petty* commodity production will have a precise historically specific element which cannot, by dint of its very nature, be stated at the primary level. Scott identifies variations in linkages and contexts which produce variant structures. This variance occurs simultaneously in its 'internal and external relations' but in each case the links can be traced from the basic elements in the primary level concept. At a further secondary level, emphasis is also placed upon sectoral differences which occur between producers. These involve particular differences in the labour process and the ways in which the *particular* means of production affect this; i.e. 'the types of relations with other forms of production and the nature of class identification and consciousness' (p .99). In the case of agricultural producers, for example, land not only provides the physical resource in establishing reproduction and property rights but it also provides a crucial basis for class relations amongst agricultural workers and producers as well as figuring large in their consciousness. It provides a basis for a whole network of social and economically dependent relations with other capitalist and non-capitalist forms. At this secondary level the actual form of production does not necessarily have to be homogeneous or pure. Specific forms of production (some more commoditised than others) may overlap but be based at the same point of production. Hence the concrete analysis of forms of production entails an analysis of all interrelations (internal and external) with all other institutions which are likely to affect its structure and trajectory of development. Consistent with Long *et al.*, (1986), and Marsden *et al.*, (1986), Scott argues that her framework:

> . . . does not imply any particular form of causality, nor does it prioritise any specific process or function. If the political, ideological and economic elements are successfully integrated into the analysis, the likely outcome will be a multiplicity of effects, with a larger space for human agency in the creation of structure, and hence of variability in the concrete manifestations of structure (p. 10).

Scott's contribution is important here in developing a theoretical and methodological path which allows higher order theory, in this case associated with petty commodity production as one mode of production, to be translated into concrete historically and spatially specific contexts. This broadens the appeal and nature of PCP, allowing it to cope more adequately with societal change.

Refreshing as this is, Scott's contribution needs to be seen in the context of the broader commoditisation approach explored by Long and his colleagues. Finding its genesis within the peasant studies literature, they attempt to apply this work in terms of the study of agrarian systems in advanced societies.

For Long *et al.*, commoditisation theory needs to go beyond 'dualistic formulations' whereby the articulation of the capitalist mode of production with other modes (e.g. PCP) are assumed to have their own internal logic of production and reproduction. Secondly, consistent with Scott's arguments, there has in the past been a lack of attention given to the *active* role of peasants, farmers and small entrepreneurs in the *process* of commoditisation. Third, they argue that there is a tendency to stress external determination which assumes a linear view of agrarian development rather than identifying the types of relationships that exist between farms, households, enterprises and various levels of external institutional structures. Rather than seeing diversity, as Bernstein suggests (1986b) as 'in need of simple concrete investigation' it is necessary to incorporate the specificity and variability of productive forms more centrally.

Indeed, in a later paper (Long and Van der Ploeg, 1988), they point to the need to decontaminate commoditisation theory from its modernisation assumptions. The assumption that there is some kind of zero starting point to development characterised by a general lack of 'commoditisation' or integration into markets needs to be abandoned. Also the assumption that the non-commoditised side of the economy progressively recedes as commoditisation proceeds, so that there is some end point to the process, fails to explain the variable significance of non-commodity relations across northern Europe and other advanced agricultures. Non-commoditised relations disappear and then re-emerge, not simply in the interstices of capitalist markets, but in their own right. As a result they help to shape and remould the accumulative tendencies of capital through time and space.

Van der Ploeg identifies major foci around which the commoditisation approach should develop. Adopting Burawoy's (1985) conception of 'regimes' of production, he focuses on the increasing influence of external agencies upon internal farm production relations. The 'scientification' of agriculture and the food chain and the increasing reliance upon 'technical–administrative relations' tie together agri-business and farm labour. In these ways, specific 'regimes' of production are created through which the real subsumption of farm labour takes place. This does not deny the significance of relations based upon petty commodity production but it places emphasis upon how they *interact* dynamically with capitals' attempts to either appropriate certain activities or monopolise the control of farm labour (see Whatmore *et al.*, 1987a and b; Marsden *et al.*, 1987) such that 'the labour process cannot be reproduced any more outside the reach of capital' (Van der Ploeg, 1986, p. 52). Scientification, or more precisely, the specific uses capital makes of science, plays a crucial role in the real subsumption of labour to capital.

Van der Ploeg (1986) provides more precise deductions emphasising the nature of social reproductive activities to the continuity of productive forms. Set in the changing context of 'commoditisation' he identifies *autonomous reproduction*, where the process of reproduction does not pass through markets and the factors of production and their inputs are not mobilised through market relations; and *market dependent reproduction* where, with the increasing 'externalisation' of tasks, reproduction demands increasing involvement with exchange. In the latter case, rather than the factors of production being primarily associated with use value, the objects of labour, instruments, and labour itself enter the process of production as commodities holding at the same time use and exchange values. Commodity relations thus penetrate the core of the process of production and begin to commoditise the labour process itself. Importantly, such processes are seen as neither unilinear nor dualistic. They produce different '*degrees*' of commoditisation over time and space. Marsden (1990) takes this a stage further by developing and adapting such models of reproduction to include the existence of pluriactivity amongst petty commodity producers. The increasing tendency for European producers to diversify production and their marketing links means that the process of reproduction of family labour and skills becomes more complex and potentially more vulnerable.

Such formulations provide useful initial framework for the study of PCP. There are at least two central issues which need to be explored, however. The first concerns the specific ways of assessing the *degree and boundaries* of commoditisation experienced by farm households in advanced economies, given that practically all forms of agrarian production and reproduction are market dependent as opposed to being reproduced autonomously. This raises the question of the validity of the commoditisation approach in assisting a more comprehensive understanding of the labour process in agriculture in advanced capitalist societies. It also entails a very careful examination of what we actually understand to be the subsumption process and its consequences for farm households.

The second, which is of equal significance, concerns the *extent of differentiation* in the commoditisation process *beyond* the farm household. Theorists admit (see Scott, 1986; Long *et al.*, 1986) that there exist high levels of differentiation in the social and economic manifestations of commodity relations on farms and that these need to be integrated into the different levels analysis associated with the dominant modes of production. Yet questions also need to be raised concerning the differentiation in the *sources* and *mediation* of the commoditisation process itself.

This suggestion contravenes much of the early Marxist writing (see Kautsky, 1900) where it was assumed that the *tendencies* in agricultural development in capitalist countries are the same everywhere, and that it was only the *form* in which such tendencies were realised that varied from one place to another. For Kautsky, for instance, variations in the realisation of tendencies could only be discovered in the differences in geographical location, climatic factors, historical conditions and the balance of political forces between different classes. Variations in the capital penetration process itself remained largely unexamined. As Hussain and Tribe (1983) point out, however:

> Kautsky completely neglects those features which are not related to the tendencies he outlines... A related consequence of the distinction adopted by Kautsky is to limit the degree to which the analysis can differentiate between the agriculture of different capitalist countries. For if the specificity of agriculture in a particular capitalist country consists in its having factors which help or hinder the realisation of tendencies which are supposedly valid for all capitalist countries, then the implication is that differences between the agricultural sector of different capitalist countries amount to them being at the different stages of realisation of the tendencies (p. 106).

In studying the commoditisation of petty commodity production and reproductive relations it is necessary to avoid restricting attention and understanding of differentiation to those actors who are based at the level of production. It is argued below that we need to challenge the assumption of the undifferentiated 'laws of motion' in the capital accumulation and commoditisation process. It is important to recognise that beyond the most abstract level at least, the sources and mediation of this process vary over time and space and are particularly influenced by and grounded in historically specific state structures which may promote and partly direct these processes (see Jessop, 1990).

The degree and boundaries of the commoditisation process

Critical to the dynamic of the agrarian commoditisation process in capitalist societies is the notion of subsumption whereby PCPs are transformed by the influence of external capital. In advanced societies, unlike in many underdeveloped countries, this is by no means a new or emergent process, but one which occurs in successive 'waves' associated with new rounds of capital penetration. For Goodman and Redclift (1986) it is seen as:

> ...the competitive movement of industrial capitals so as to create sectors of valorisation by restructuring the inherited 'pre-industrial' labour process (p. 45).

Industrial capital, in this sense, has successively appropriated parts of production previously associated with the farm (see Goodman *et al.*, 1987). Levels of *real* subsumption have, however, been largely restricted to certain sectors such as intensive livestock and poultry production in northern Europe. Industrial capital has largely been constrained, principally through the natural and land-based nature of agricultural production, only succeeding where advancements in science and technology weaken such constraints. For Goodman and Redclift, the degree and limits of commoditisation are largely restricted to the levels of real subsumption that have been developed either by industrial substitutes for agricultural products or, more widely, by the appropriation of parts of the original agricultural labour process (Goodman and Redclift, 1986).

For Van der Ploeg such a restricted conception of real subsumption, based solely upon economic principles, ignores many important features. The 'remaining tasks' supposedly untouched by this process are not left unaffected. Even where levels of real subsumption are limited, farm households are influenced indirectly by external agencies. Through forcing upon producers and their families in an increasingly competitive context, a more rationalistic, scientific mode of operation the demands of real subsumption are further satisfied *despite* the constraints to which Goodmann and Redclift allude. For Van der Ploeg (1986), real subsumption is more embracing and uneven than the concepts of appropriation and substitution would suggest:

> Real subsumption of agricultural labour arises not so much where capital 'appropriates' certain activities, but where it starts to monopolise the *control* of the labour process on the farm such that this labour process cannot be reproduced any more outside the reach of capital (p. 52).

Such a broadening of the subsumption notion accommodates considerable variability of production and reproductive relations in agrarian change, focusing on the indirect means by which external capitals seek to control the labour process.

Whatmore *et al.*, (1987b) and Marsden *et al.*, (1987) also argue, in a longitudinal study of farm businesses in lowland England, that whilst the examination of the consequences of subsumption (as outlined by Van der Ploeg) provide important new insights, the process is highly variable both over time and space. They focus upon the changes in the internal organisation of farm businesses, and in particular the increasing diffusion of control away from the farm family in terms of farm capital, ownership, land rights, business management structure and labour relations. Over 20 per cent of the sampled farms experienced an increase in the subsumption of internal relations, i.e. where farm families had decreased their independent control over farm business assets and their management, labour supply and land rights of the farm. The study indicated first a degree of stability of farm businesses in terms of their internal relations over the relatively short study period (1970–85), but second a clear directional shift towards the increasing diffusion of control for nearly a third of the sample. This represented a move towards more corporate, complex farm business organisations, technical arrangements, multi-unit enterprises and complex labour profiles employing a variety of types of labour. The owner-occupation of farms, the conventional renting of land and sole ownership of the farm business assets became less attractive options to the survival of farm families over the study period. In the Metropolitan Green Belt (around London) and in the

Bedfordshire study area (an area of large-scale cereal growing) the diffusion of control was associated with the necessity to intensify and capitalise farm businesses in order to maintain returns. Also the introduction of new forms of capital taxation in the 1970s and the changes in the relative rates of return from particular agricultural and off farm activities was influential.

The uneven patterns of subsumption over time also showed different tendencies occurring between the three study areas. For instance, in West Dorset, an area of small dairy farms, more farms had remained static over the study period with a significantly larger proportion (11.5%) experiencing lower levels of subsumption. For a small minority there was an *increasing* reliance upon family ownership and labour representing a form of *social marginalisation* based upon a lack of opportunities to incorporate other family members into the business, and a resistance to terminate independent family interests in agricultural land and capital completely, at least in the short term.

While all such assessments of the temporal and spatial variability of the subsumption process are highly dependent upon the relative sensitivity of the indicators developed, such evidence at least gives clues as to the nature of change at the farm household level. This is a result both of the interaction of the broad structural changes associated with the tendential movement of capital *and* the specific compromises and strategies (both short term and long term) farm families pursue.

Whilst much of this work attempts to assess the levels of subsumption it does not sufficiently explore how commodity relations are mediated *within* the farm family, or how they interact with or provide a basis for social and ideological frameworks. For instance, one problem with Van der Ploeg's models of market dependent reproduction is that they beg the questions: what constitutes non-commoditised household and kinship relations in advanced capitalist agriculture? And what degree of commoditisation occurs in the processes of reproduction? The lines between commodified and non-commodified relations in the sphere of reproduction are indeed blurred and necessitate more theoretical and methodological effort. For instance, the common assumptions which relegate domestic labour as a 'service' to the effective reproduction of *production* tend to ignore the central question of the material and ideological dimensions of familial gender relations and how these construct and modify the 'roles' men and women perform across generations. For Friedmann (1986b):

> Men and women battle to preserve both small property and the patriarchal family as the only institutions in their experience, real or imaginary, which give concrete expression to desires for independence and for social relations based on generosity and respect. Both needs are constricted and distorted by patriarchal and capitalist relations, yet once both the family household and small property are constantly threatened, such needs are easily translated into recurrent struggles to preserve what are seen as the last and only 'surviving' bases of a 'way of life' as the farmers say, in contrast to the ruthless world of a business (p. 41).

There is a danger here of translating the dualisms associated with the arguments about capitalist and petty commodity modes of production beyond the farm door to the analysis of internal family dynamics. Considerable disagreement exists as to what precisely constitutes 'reproduction' of the farm household (see O'Hara, 1987) particularly with regard to its direct role for maintaining production (see Friedmann, 1986; Delphy, 1977; Whatmore, 1991). However, a central focus must concern the interaction of gender and generational relations as social relations *in their own right* and the ways these interact with production and commodity relations. The process by which the reproduction of social and commodity relations become separated and re-integrated over time must be a central focus for those concerned with further developing an understanding of commoditisation. Friedmann's (1986b) definition of reproduction as:

> The renewal from one round of production to another of the social and technical elements of production and of the relations among them (p.162) would seem too restrictive here.

The sources and mediation of commodity relations

The recent literature concerning the commoditisation process as it affects petty commodity producers in particular has yet to fully incorporate a more comprehensive understanding of the varied methods adopted by fractions of financial and industrial capital in transforming the family based labour process. This demands focusing attention upon the *competitive movement of capital* mediated through financial institutions and agro-industrial firms *and then* assessing the consequences of this at the level of farm production. Considerable emphasis is now being given to the significance of fractions of industrial capital (see Goodman *et al.*, 1987; Buttel *et al.*, 1983; Wallace 1985; Ward, 1990) and, in particular, to the ways technological and biotechnological innovation is transforming the production process in agriculture (Goodman and Wilkinson, 1990). However, the workings of fractions of finance capital and the variability in the exploitative relations which exist between financial institutions, farm input suppliers, food processors and retailers and the farm based sector have yet to be fully understood.

Some of the American sociological literature is focusing attention on these issues. Green (1984), for example, has examined the consequences of the gradual centralisation and deregulation of the US banking systems for American agriculture, linking the structure of credit provision to the access and cost of credit itself at the farm level. Mooney (1986) attempts to identify cycles of change whereby farm indebtedness and tenancy replace one another with credit-based production being seen as an ephemeral phenomenon. Mooney (1988) attempts to conceptualise finance capital in the United States whereby reciprocal, but not necessarily equal, relationships exist between indebted producers and the credit market. There is also an important role for the state in determining the structure of the market. The deregulation of the banking sectors in the US, the UK, and more recently, France is engendering new sets of relations between credit suppliers and farmers, encouraging in some cases further family based self-exploitation and the further reduction of hired labour. The use of credit transforms not only the social relations of agricultural production but also the structure of the food chain (see Marsden *et al.*, 1990a). The provision of credit provides the 'lubricant' for the capital intensification process which, at the very least, necessitates the substitution of capital for labour and its deplacement from the farm to the industrial input sector (e.g. the manufacturing of tractors, chemicals etc). More significant, and consistent with Van der Ploeg's conception of 'scientification', are the ways in which credit agencies determine what *loans are used for* and *who is credit worthy*. This provides credit agencies with considerable control over the type and direction of capital 'intensification'. In terms of the *type* of intensification, Mooney argues that it has stimulated farmers to produce more cash *volume* rather than production efficiency *per se*, tending to promote the increasing scale of production and intensification of agriculture. Selection procedures aim at pin-pointing those who wish to farm for profit-maximisation. This involves scrutinising farm families for their potential for petty accumulation and abilities to withstand reduced levels of domestic consumption.

Considerable differences occur, however, in the ways in which the competitive fractions of capital impinge upon farm based production between, and indeed to a certain extent within, national boundaries. Marsden *et al.*, (1990), through the collection of case study evidence in Britain, have conducted an investigation of key agencies and organisations operating in the wider agro-industrial complex (including input suppliers, credit suppliers, food manufacturers and retailers). This assesses the ways in which these agencies exert an increasingly important influence over the farm sector through the supply of credit, advanced technology and associated advice and through marketing contracts.

A restructuring of the food complex took place in Britain during the 1980s mainly as a consequence of the falling farm incomes and the increased competition this has generated for market share. The evidence illustrates, first, the variability of relations that credit suppliers, input manufacturers and retailers hold with farmers and, second, the considerable adjustments made in the competitive strategies of the financial and industrial companies. A major feature of the UK system is that whilst transnational companies operate in the agro-inputs and food processing sectors they have not become directly involved in the farm production process via subsidiary companies. However, the credit suppliers, input suppliers, processors and retailers are highly oligopolistic in character. For instance, three companies control 95 per cent of the agricultural fertiliser market, four control 77 per cent of agro-machinery and three 90 per cent of the UK frozen food market (see Ward, 1990). Four major clearing banks dominate the agricultural credit market.

The growth in concentration has increased rapidly since the 1960s. The process of restructuring takes a form partly derived from the necessity for technological development. Small, independent companies operating in the high risk sectors of the markets create and invest in specialist niches exploiting new technological processes or products. The more successful and profitable of these companies become absorbed into the corporate network of the dominant multinationals through takeover and merger. This reduces the expense of risk of research and development for the larger firms, enabling them to rationalise production capacity by closing older, less efficient plants (see Marsden and Little, 1990).

Faced with these competitive movements in the agro-industrial complex, actual farm production increasingly becomes the weakest link in the food chain. Price and income inelasticities associated with basic food demand exacerbate the competition in the food chain, promoting higher value added versions of existing food products. This does little to stimulate direct demand at the farm gate thereby depressing further the prices of major farm commodities and income.

In the late 1980s, therefore, several major changes in the linkages between farm based production and external capital (in the form of input suppliers, credit suppliers, food processors and retailers) can be identified. While in a general sense these represent new rounds of commoditisation and scientification for agricultural producers, the tendencies are made more varied by the competing and changing strategies external capital adopts in its attempts to maintain levels of surplus value from engaging in the food production process. Also, as we noted in our discussions about subsumption earlier, they are affected by the abilities and inabilities of specific farm households to *adapt* to these changing demands. There are five major features:

(1) The restructuring of credit provision has occurred owing to a rapid rise in farm debts and in particular 'core' debt. Over the period 1976–86 total farm debts rose by £2.4 million to £8.5 million, which in terms of debt-to-asset ratios represented an increase of 9.9 per cent to 18.5 per cent. During the same period farm income halved and the payments of interest absorbed over three times the proportion of farm income (9% in 1976, 31% in 1985). Banks have revised their blanket policies of lending on the basis of security against land assets to a more complex farm by farm system which relates directly to the profitability and future viability of the farm enterprise. One feature of this has been a reduction in the proportion of agricultural lending on overdraft to more tightly defined credit plans and schemes.

(2) Increasing links have developed between financial institutions selling credit and the input suppliers. The demand for farm inputs such as fertilisers and machinery has been declining as farmers themselves have reduced inputs in response to falling farm incomes. This has promoted intense competition in the input suppliers' markets, manifesting itself either in terms of price cutting between major companies or the establishment of 'credit packages' for farmers often made in collaboration with the large lending institutions. Input suppliers are then able to offer farmers a variety of 'credit service plans' on concessionary rates of interest which stimulate sales and maintain market share. Farmers are faced with an increasing array of hire

purchase agreements, leases, contract hires and simple cash purchase schemes (e.g. credit for fertilisers).

(3) The development of such credit packages either with banks alone or in conjunction with input suppliers serves to increase the direct levels and variety of advice given to farmers. From technical services (e.g. soil survey analysis, irrigation scheduling and dairy costing programmes) to farm business planning, the use and action taken on such advice is made a condition of loan packages. More conditions are being placed upon the farmers who enter agreements (see also Mooney, 1986), while the distribution of credit is also becoming more selective.

(4) The transfer of agricultural inputs from suppliers to producers is, in itself, an increasingly competitive process which demands more direct marketing with producers at the local level. Increasingly strong directive control is placed upon local dealers which is enforced through differentiated incentive and bonus systems, implemented at the head office and regional level.

(5) The large retailing multiples exercise growing power over the farming sector as well as food processing. They are increasingly by-passing the wholesale commodity markets and purchasing direct on contract from farmers. The specifications in contracts to producers are detailed and supported by technical advice placing strong emphasis upon quality control. This not only has a direct influence upon the labour organisation of farms (particularly the progressive casualisation of labour for peak planting and harvest periods) but it also indirectly stimulates the input and credit suppliers markets within the farm production sector. Moreover, the rise in retailer brand names of products weakens the competitive position of established food processors, whose products become increasingly more expensive for the consumer.

The decline in farm incomes and capital stock as well as the increasing debt burdens of farmers in Britain are leading to more intensive and diversified efforts on the part of input and credit suppliers and retailers to exploit the agricultural production process. While different fractions are in competition with one another to maintain their market share, the advantages of specific collaboration for the purposes of developing new forms of credit package have been discovered. Moreover, unlike the situation in the US, British banks are highly oligopolistic and their agricultural lending remains relatively low (7% approximately). These tendencies are doing little to reduce the processes of subsumption of production at the farm level. Nevertheless, as some of the evidence already outlined demonstrates, not all farmers are attracted to increasing their linkages with these external agencies. Some may *progressively resist* the attractions of marketing contracts, credit packages and receiving technical and financial advice even though this may lead to further self-exploitation of family labour and the eventual collapse of the business itself. From the point of view of credit and input suppliers, however, the farm production sector represents a highly segmented market, the growth of which is dependent upon pursuing the economics of intensification and the progressive concentration of production amongst fewer 'business oriented' and 'programmable' farm families.

Conclusion: redefining a new agenda

The later arguments developed here explore some of the potentialities and problems associated with the commoditisation debate, in the context of the persistence of petty commodity production. It is recognised that there is a need to go beyond debates concerning the articulation of modes of production (i.e. petty commodity production vis-à-vis capitalist production) and to focus more intuitively upon the variable sets of interactions which occur between external capitals and households, grounded as they are within specific nation state structures and culturally specific contexts. In Europe such interactions in commodity relations are strongly influenced by state policy which has, through a variety of agricultural and fiscal instruments, provided a context which encourages both the concentration of farm production and, at the same time, its increasing exploitation by financial institutions and food firms. Whilst some aspects of state policy may be gradually changing direction towards more extensive, environmentally sensitive farm policies (for example, quotas, levies, and set aside schemes) this is doing little to deter private capital from increasingly promoting intensification and technological change. It may be, as Friedmann suggests, that it is upon those less commoditised, familial and patriarchal relations that increasing numbers of petty commodity producers will have to rely if they are to protect both their forms and, indeed, actual mode of production.

Implicit in what has been argued here is the need to integrate more centrally, both in theoretical and empirical terms, petty commodity production within our wider analyses of rural change. Whilst its existence may seem to contradict long standing assumptions concerning proletarianisation, value relations, concentration of private property and ownership of the means of production, a focus upon the web of dependent relations between, as well as within, PCPs and other economic and political sectors suggests more complex logics in agrarian development than had previously been appreciated. It has been argued that the position of PCP should be seen as complementary to the development of more sophisticated forms of economic activity and that at various historical junctures and places the emergence of PCP as a dynamic and transforming force, *in itself*, becomes a central element in rural development and change (see Morvaridi, 1990). In this sense its very nature, both in an abstract sense and in terms of its diverse grounded conditions (see Scott, J., 1986), is an important agent in the process of uneven development over time and space. Gender and generation, through a process of production and reproduction may seem to contradict the goals of the capitalist market, but at base they tend to reinforce it. The progressive decline in small petty producers in rural areas does not in itself negate the relevance of family exploitation overall in the agrarian systems of advanced societies. As Gasson *et al.* (1988) note, for instance, the 'capitalisation' of agriculture has not necessarily reduced the importance of the family or inter family relationships in serving as a basis for continuity and ideology. Moreover the ideologies of the family and business are not by any means opposed (see Hutson, 1987).

The salience of these suggestions should be seen in the context of a need to confront more clearly aspects of uneven development in capitalist societies over time and space. Once one moves away from unilinear assumptions concerning the nature of agrarian development, as for instance represented by the processes of proletarianisation, it is possible to accommodate the tendencies in petty commodity production to re-emerge and evolve under particular social, political and economic conditions. It may not do this as an independent entity within its own continuous internal unity. Its expression will be highly differentiated, potentially flexible but inextricably tied to the sets of commodity and non commodity relations which surround it. The support given by transnational and national state structures not only to land based agricultural production but also to long-standing notions of private property rights can, in combination, provide the conditions for the social and economic reproduction of PCPs, even if this means an absolute decline in their number and an increasing pressure for them to diversify their production and marketing relations (see Marsden and Murdoch, 1990). Whilst they may suffer the problems of increasing vulnerability and marginalisation at the national and international scale, this represents in many cases the very social means around which economic and political struggles are based. Their very social adaptability, based as it is on patriarchal gender relations and a variety of types of self-exploitation and succession, provides the basis for uneven and hard won micro-social trajectories. In aggregate terms these will represent regional, local and national diversity in rural development, and thus provide the preconditions for new uneven rounds of capital penetration.

It is, though, at this juncture, that we find current research and debate so lacking in that there are few attempts to examine these dynamics in their local or regional settings and to explore the multiplicity of commodity links associated with PCPs (but see Sage in chapter 4; Paloscia in chapter 3, and Kovach in chapter 5). Moreover, the extent to which petty commodity producers develop and reproduce class consciousness and methods of political mediation so as to aid their risky sustainability is far from illuminated. As a consequence it would seem that the times are right for a reinvigorated examination of petty commodity production, particularly from a comparative perspective. This will need to avoid the dualities and assumptions of the past and attempt to produce frameworks which incorporate different levels of abstraction and contextualisation within and beyond national boundaries.

References

Banaji, J. (1977) Summary of selected parts of Kautsky's *The Agrarian Question, Economy and society* 5, 1:2–49.

Benton, T. (1984) *The Rise and Fall of Structural Marxism: Althusser and his influence*. London, Macmillan.
Bernstein, H. (1986a) Is there a concept of petty commodity production generic to capitalism? Paper presented to the thirteenth European congress of Rural Sociology, Braga, Portugal.
Bernstein, H. (1986b) Capitalism and petty commodity production, *Social Analysis 20*.
Billings, D. and Tickamyer, A. (1990) Development and Underdevelopment: The Politics of Region. Conference paper. American Rural Sociological Association. Norfolk, Virginia.
Bonnano, A. (1990) *Agrarian Policies and Agricultural Systems*. Colorado, Westview Press.
Burawoy, M. (1985) *The Politics of Production*. London, New Left Books, (Verso).
Buttel, F. (1982) The political economy of agriculture in advanced industrial societies, *Current perspectives in social theory* 3:27–55.
Buttel, F. H., Kloppenburg, J., Kenney, M. and Cowan, H. T. (1983) Genetic engineering and the restructuring of agricultural research, *The Rural Sociologist* 3: 132–44.
Chayanov, A. V. (1925) *The Theory of Peasant Economy*. Translated by D. Thorner, R. E. F. Smith and B. Kerblay Irwin, 1966.
Chevalier, J. (1983) There is nothing simple about simple commodity production, *Journal of Peasant Studies* 10: 153–86.
Cochrane, W. (1979) *The development of American Agriculture: a historical analysis*. Minneapolis, University of Minnesota Press.
Davis, J. E. (1980) Capitalist agricultural development and the exploitation of the propertied labourer, in Buttel, F. and Newby, H. (1980) *Rural Sociology of advanced societies*. New Jersey, Montclair.
Delphy, C. (1977) *The main enemy*. London, Women's Research and Resources Centre.
FitzSimmons, M. (1986) The new industrial agriculture; the regional integration of speciality crop production, *Economic Geography*, 62, 4:334–53.
Friedmann, H. (1980) Household production and the national economy: concepts for the analysis of agrarian primations, *Journal of Peasant Studies* 7 (2):158–84.
Friedmann, H. (1982) The family farm in advanced capitalism: Outline of a theory of simple commodity production in agriculture. Conference paper to the American Sociological Association, Toronto.
Friedmann, H. (1986a) Patriarchy and Property: a reply to Goodman and Redclift, *Sociologia Ruralis* XXVI: 2.
Friedmann, H. (1986b) Patriarchal Commodity Production, *Social Analysis* 10, December.
Galeski, B. and Wilkening, E. (1987) *Studies in Family Farming*. New York, Westview Press.
Gasson, R. *et al.* (1988) The farm as a family business: a review, *Journal of Agricultural Economics*, 39: 1–41.

Goodman, D. and Redclift, M. (1986) Capitalism, petty commodity production and the farm enterprise, *Sociologia Ruralis* XXV: 3/4.

Goodman, D., Sorj, and Wilkinson, J. (1987) *From Farming to Biotechnology*. Oxford, Basil Blackwell.

Goodman, D. and Wilkinson, J. (1990) Patterns of research and innovation in the modern agro-food system, in Lowe, P., Marsden, T. and Whatmore, S. *Technological change and the Rural Environment*. London, David Fulton Publishers.

Green, G. P. (1984) Credit and agriculture: Some Consequences of the centralisation of the banking system, *Rural Sociology* 49, 4: 568–79.

Hussain, A. and Tribe, K. (1983) *Marxism and the agrarian question*. London, Macmillan.

Hutson, J. (1987) Fathers and sons: family farms, family businesses and the farming industry, *Sociology* 21: 215–31.

Jessop, B. (1990) Regulation theories in retrospect and prospect, *Economy and Society* 19, 2: 154–216.

Kautsky, K. (1900) *Die Agrarfrage*. Dietz, Stuttgart.

Long, N., Van der Ploeg, J., Curtin, C. and Box, L. (1986) *The Commoditisation debate: labour process, strategy and social network*. Working paper, University of Wageningen.

Long, N. and Van der Ploeg, J. (1988) New challenges in the sociology of Rural Development: a rejoinder to Peter Vandergeest, *Sociologia Ruralis*, 18, 1:30–42.

Mann, S. and Dickenson, J. (1980) State and agriculture in two eras of American capitalism, in Buttel, F. and Newby, H. (eds) *The rural sociology of advanced societies*. New Jersey, Montclair.

Mann, S. (1990) *Agrarian Change: Theory and Practice*. University of North Carolina Press.

Mandel, E. L. (1978) *The second slump*. London, New Left Books.

Marsden, T. K. and Little, J. (eds) (1990) *Political, Social and Economic Perspectives on the International Food System*. Aldershot, Averbury.

Marsden, T. K., Munton, R. J., Whatmore, S. J. and Little, J. K. (1986) Towards a political economy of capitalist agriculture: a British perspective, *International Journal and Regional Research* 4.

Marsden, T. K. and Murdoch, J. (1990) Agriculture in retreat: implications for the control and development of rural land, *Countryside Change Initiative Working Paper*, No. 9. London.

Marsden, T. K., Whatmore, S. J. and Munton, R. J. C. (1987) Uneven Development and the Restructuring Process in British Agriculture: a preliminary exploration, *Journal of Rural Studies*, 4.

Marsden, T. K., Whatmore, S. and Munton, R. (1990a) Finance capital and the food complex. Chapter 2 in Marsden, T. K. and Little, J. K. (eds) *Political, Social and Economic Perspectives on the International Food System*. Aldershot, Averbury.

Marsden, T. K., Lowe, P. and Whatmore, S. (1990b) (eds) *Rural Restructuring*. Critical Perspectives on Rural Change Series, Volume 1, Chapter 1.

Marsden, T. K. (1990) Towards a political economy of Pluriactivity, *Journal of Rural Studies*, special issue.
Mooney, P. H. (1986) The political economy of credit in American Agriculture, *Rural Sociology*, 51, 4: 449–70.
Mooney, P. H. (1988) *My Own Boss?* New York, Westview Press.
Morvaridi, B. (1990) Strategies of households in the production of cash/food crops, in Marsden, T. K. and Little, J. *Political, Social and Economic Perspectives on the International Food System*. Aldershot, Averbury.
Munton, R. J. C. and Marsden, T. K. (1990) Dualism or diversity in family farming? Patterns of occupancy change in British agriculture, *Geoforum*.
Newby, H. (1987) Emerging Issues in theories of agrarian development, *Arkelton Trust occasional paper 2*.
O'Hara, P. (1987) Inside the black box: the need to explore the internal dynamics of family farms. Paper presented to Arkelton Trust meeting, Montpelier, June 1987.
Scott, A. M. (1986) Towards a rethinking of Petty Commodity Production, *Social analysis*, 20.
Scott, J. (1986) *Capitalist Property and Financial Power*. London, Wheatsheaf.
Smith, C. (1986) Reconstructing the elements of petty commodity production, *Social Analysis*, No. 20, December.
Van der Ploeg, J. (1986) Chapter in Long *et al. The commoditisation debate*. University of Wageningen.
Wallace, I. (1985) Towards a geography of agribusiness, *Progress in Human Geography*, 9:411–514.
Ward, N. (1990) A preliminary analysis of the UK food chain, *Food Policy* 15: 439–41.
Whatmore, S., Munton, R., Marsden, T. and Little, J. (1987a) Towards a typology of farm businesses in contemporary British agriculture, *Sociologia Ruralis*, XXVII 1: 21–37.
Whatmore, S., Munton, R., Marsden, T. and Little J. (1987b) Interpreting a relational typology of farm businesses in Southern England, *Sociologia Ruralis*, XXVII, 2/3: 103–22.
Whatmore, S. (1991) *Farming Women: gender, work and family enterprise*. Basingstoke, Macmillan.

CHAPTER 3

Agriculture and Diffused Manufacturing in the Terza Italia: *A Tuscan Case-Study*

Raffaele Paloscia

Introduction

The development of small enterprise in Italy, particularly in those regions where it is the most characteristic form of production, has raised a great deal of interest at an international level. The reason for this lies in the economic success Italy has enjoyed over recent decades, largely due to the spread and consolidation in the so-called *Terza Italia* (Third Italy) of a production system based on an interconnected range of small manufacturing firms. This production system has been seen by numerous scholars as an alternative model for industrial development to mass production, which is now experiencing serious difficulties. It is taken as a very good example of what is defined as flexible specialisation.[1] Perhaps less well known, because they have been less fully explored by the various foreign authors who have written about the *Terza Italia*, are the connections that exist between the development of small enterprise and certain characteristics typical of the areas in which it has thrived. More specifically, there are clear elements of continuity between the new territorial formation - defined as 'urbanised countryside' - derived from diffused industrial development strongly mixed with agricultural activity, and the original rural society strongly marked by its socio-cultural, economic and spatial orders.

The object of this article is to enlarge on this theme, taking Tuscany, a key area in Italy's new productive context, as a specific example. We will examine the processes which have led from a dualistic interpretation of Italian development to the more comprehensive view contained in the definition of the *Terza Italia*. We will then outline its special characteristics, in particular the economic and social ones, which make it so different from both the north and the south of Italy. To show how this particular territorial formation came into being we will identify some basic prerequisites, which will then be analysed from the point of view of Tuscan *mezzadria* (share-cropping). This will allow us to focus on the deep-seated, historically determined roots of the links between the agricultural and industrial activities which characterise the region and which have formed the basis of its economic growth in the last few decades. This development will be examined in its socio-economic and territorial components, with the rural areas and the farming families settled in them at the centre of the analysis; we will trace the various stages of their progressive involvement in the process of diffusion of industrial activity, touching on some more recent changes which offer a glimpse of possible future developments. Some final considerations will sum up the article's main points, relating them both to some theoretical positions concerning the *Terza Italia* and what novelties emerge from a broader context.

From two Italys to three

Up until the early seventies any analysis of economic development in Italy was based on a traditional dualistic view, widely accepted by scholars, regardless of their political ideology or school of historic, or economic, thought. This view divided Italy very schematically into two large geographical areas: the North, industrialised and rich, an integral part of economically advanced continental Europe; and the South, still agricultural and poor, characterised by a general backwardness.[2] Differences in interpreting this situation lay mainly in defining the economic and political relationship between the two areas and in laying the blame for the persistent lack of balance.

Within this framework the areas between North and South were of secondary importance, and considered rather static in comparison to the dynamics of both the 'industrial triangle' (Lombardy, Piedmont and Liguria), and Southern Italy and the islands.

A single statistic is enough to explain this interpretation: between 1951 and 1971 more than 4 million people emigrated from the South, the population of which was around 18 million in 1951. Many emigrants went abroad, going overseas in the period straight after the war and, later, to the more industrialised countries of Europe, such as Germany and Switzerland. However, the majority of these emigrants, particularly during the economic boom at the end of the fifties and during the early sixties, moved to the regions in the north-west of Italy.[3] Nearly all the emigrants were young males from the agricultural sector, highly sought after by the factories in Milan and Turin. Thus, while the economic and social structure in the South was irremediably broken down and rural areas abandoned[4], the production of 'wealth' became concentrated in the great cities of the North.

The vertically integrated factory was the mainstay of this extraordinary industrial growth, just as it was all over Europe after the war: thousands, sometimes tens of thousands, of workers were gathered under a single roof and organised around a vast production chain, which issued forth ever increasing quantities of finished products with growing economies of scale. The concentration of capital and the work force in the big cities led to an urban and territorial organisation that completely conformed to industrial rhythms and methods of production. Such territorial formations served a series of indispensable functions outside the moment of production in a strict sense. Thus the so-called *città fabbrica*[5] came into being, together with a model of metropolitan development which was responsible for energy waste and problems at an environmental level which have become vital questions in our own times.

However, the *città fabbrica* (factory-city) was not destined to last for long. The warning signs of the crisis were already visible towards the end of the *miracolo economico* (economic boom): the new political climate in the early sixties, with socialists in the government for the first time and a much more active union movement in the big factories in the North, led to the workers' success in obtaining substantial wage increases.

The years of economic crisis (1963–65) slowed the situation somewhat, but the question of redistributing profits in favour of an increasingly aware working class came to the fore once more with the substantial recovery of the economy and throughout the subsequent 'hot' years between 1969 and 1972. Alongside wage claims, insistent demands were made regarding much broader social needs, from better working conditions to the right to adequate housing and more efficient services, for all of which it was held big business should be responsible. In this way the mechanism of accumulation that had been built on the organisational structure of the *città fabbrica* was shackled.

The fuel crisis provided another decisive destabilising factor for industrial conglomerations. It affected the organisation of production profoundly at an international level from 1973 on, completely altering raw material exchange relations. The unexpected rise in fuel costs, particularly in the cost of the main source of energy used in Italian industry,[6] together with the already increased cost of labour, brought about a progressive and overall decline in profits for large companies.

The new strategy developed by entrepreneurs to regain control of production factors, particularly of labour, and to return to margins of profit no longer feasible under existing conditions, was to decentralise production. Briefly, this meant breaking down the production cycle into a number of separate parts and sending them outside the factory. Many new companies were created, or older ones adapted (generally characterised by being very small), to carry out just one phase in the production cycle, often the manufacture of a single component. The phases crucial for increasing capital, particularly those relating to getting the finished product into the marketplace, remained in the hands of the parent company.

This strategy created a major shift away from the industrial concentrations in the north-west, where relations between labour and capital had become very rigid. Other areas came to the fore within the country (although for some specific production cycles, also outside the country), with special characteristics more suited to the flexible needs of the new production mode. The ways in which the productive apparatus in Italy was restructured in this direction, the new importance of the small business, the variety of businesses and intercompany relations and the dynamics they have given rise to in the different areas, and industrial relations, have created a highly articulated and very complex situation. Much has been written on the subject, both in Italy and abroad, since the beginning of the seventies.[7]

In the years since then applied research and the refinement of theories have outlined, within the general context described, a new territorial formation with characteristics quite distinct both from the traditional areas of Italian development and the backward South. For its peculiar structural elements and geographical delimitation, Bagnasco defined this area as the *Terza Italia*, marking the end of the dualistic interpretation of Italian development.[8]

The Terza Italia and the 'urbanised countryside'

What are the distinctive features of the economy of the *Terza Italia* as Bagnasco identified them in his study of the situation in the mid-seventies (Bagnasco, 1977: 153–69)? The overall predominance of small businesses within the industrial structure of the particular regions and the importance of traditional manufacturing (textiles, footwear, clothing, tanning and leather work, wood, furniture, ceramics) are fundamental features of the *Terza Italia*. Another distinctive element is the very high quota of exports, with respect to the national average of around 20 per cent, on the total of the entire production, often with privileged relations between specific regions and foreign countries.[9] Furthermore, agriculture retains, at least in some areas, quite important production functions. Tourism, mainly foreign, is also enormously important for the entire economy and is far more widespread than in the north-west or south. This, then, is the general picture. But what is it that has distinguished the *Terza Italia* in the evolution of its industrial structure?

According to Bagnasco, the marginal economy of southern Italy owes it backwardness not so much to the lack of industrial installations – although they are in short supply – as to the haphazard aggregation of different scales of production; a haphazardness effectively preventing the formation of a necessary productive matrix. The opposite is true in the developed areas of the North where production activities exist in integrated systems based on the model of large business/small satellite business, in a clearly dependent relationship. In contrast, while production in the *Terza Italia* is highly integrated, this is not induced by large companies, but is the result of the aggregation of small, varied and specialised production activities. These can range from the spatial aggregation of related businesses on the basis of a purely imitative mechanism, to highly articulated networks with intricate and variable inter-company relations which give rise to complete productive cycles, although split and spread out over the area. In this context industrial relations are very flexible, thanks to the interweaving of work relationships with personal and family ones. While this gives rise to a more conscious job participation, it also often means rates of pay, hours and working conditions well below legal standards.

Spatially, the productive structures tend to be concentrated in given areas, making a sort of leopard skin of the map of the *Terza Italia* of the seventies. An initial list of the most evolved 'spots' was worked out by Garofoli, who also attempted to reconstruct their common constitutive elements in his felicitous definition of a 'system-area'.[10] The specific characteristics that make a 'system-area' of a given productive zone have been summarised by Garofoli as follows:

(1) the importance of the area at a national level for the production quota of its particular specialisation;
(2) the existence of numerous small and medium-sized businesses which are interdependent, although without a 'leader' business;
(3) a distinct production specialisation in one or more sectors pivoted around a single product;
(4) other specific characteristics, such as a labour force with diffused skills, high job mobility and elevated rates of job turnover; the existence, therefore, of an articulated social structure associated with high levels of mobility.

This final characteristic is linked to prerequisites which are not strictly speaking economic, but more generally socio-cultural; they permit a given area to build up the necessary energy and, at a given moment, to trigger off a development mechanism based on small industry and decentralisation, or rather, productive diffusion. Reducing these prerequisites to their two essential elements, they can be identified as the availability of a labour force with an agricultural background derived from a rural community with its peculiar characteristics, and a consolidated and widespread artisan tradition in specific production sectors. While these two elements are common to the experience of local development in central, north and east Italy, they take on distinctive connotations in the different regions and, sometimes, sub-regions.

To refine the analysis, particularly the interrelations that have been established between the rural world and the productive system based on small enterprise, we need to examine these two elements as they relate to Tuscany, an important region of the *Terza Italia*. These have been clearly identified in Tuscany, by the studies carried out since the end of the sixties, as constitutive features of a new territorial formation, defined as 'urbanised countryside'.[11]

Mezzadria and the artisan tradition in Tuscany

Tuscany provides a good example of recent development based on small enterprise and diffused industrialisation; it also provides an excellent example of the interweaving, from many points of view, of the rural and urban worlds. The continual, often conflict-ridden, exchange of human energy, capital and cultural models between these diverse realities has left its mark on the rich history of the region, bringing about special forms of economic development and social and territorial formation. In Tuscany (or more precisely, the vast area of the basin of the Arno and some smaller rivers in the south-east of the region) the two prerequisites for the development of the distinctive industrial formation of the *Terza Italia* can be traced to the prevalence of a particular form of agricultural organisation - the *mezzadria* - and the widespread concentrations of artisan work and cottage industry, in numerous urban centres of ancient origin.

The *mezzadria* consisted[12] of an agricultural contract - in theory an annual agreement although in practice it lasted much longer - between a landowner and a cultivator, the latter becoming a *mezzadro* on the basis of the contract. Under this agreement the landowner provided the *mezzadro* with a plot of land, the *podere* (farm), and a house to live in, along with various agricultural outbuildings. In return the *mezzadro* agreed to cultivate the land, guaranteeing the use of the labour force of his entire family, and also carried out various other jobs for the landowner, such as ploughing and planting new crops, maintenance of the landowner's house, etc. The expenses involved in running the *podere* and the final product were divided equally between the two. From its beginnings the *mezzadria* constituted a central and constant factor not only of the economy, but more generally of the society and way of life in the region. Its origins date back to the breakdown of the feudal system when the new urban landowners, having abolished serfdom, tied the serfs to the land once more with share-cropping agreements. However, these agreements are generally considered as the first step towards more modern types of agrarian relationships (Sereni, 1984: 173–4).

Thus, the *mezzadria* was founded from the city which, during the course of its long history, would draw capital and skills in a cyclic series of interrelationships of which the recent spread to rural areas of small manufacturing, associated with a crisis in the large urban factory, can be seen as the latest expression. The eighteenth century crisis in urban manufacturing and related international trade (in which the cities of Tuscany were leaders) led to the introduction of reforms abolishing the encumbrances on much of the land and draining vast areas of poor terrain. This involved the injection of urban capital into the share-cropping countryside and gave rise to a more articulated form of agricultural production based on the *fattoria* (farm) (Sereni, 1984: 237).

The *fattoria* contained the house of the *fattore*, who represented the landowner in relations with the share-croppers and carried out the functions of administration and overseeing. From the *fattoria* were dispensed other functions more directly related to production (processing or preservation plants for some products, commonly used machinery and tools, etc.). As the management organisation of the great noble estates subdivided into numerous share-cropping *poderi*, the *fattoria* became the controlling element of the new economic, social, and spatial order of the share-cropping world which was essential for the development of diffused manufacturing.

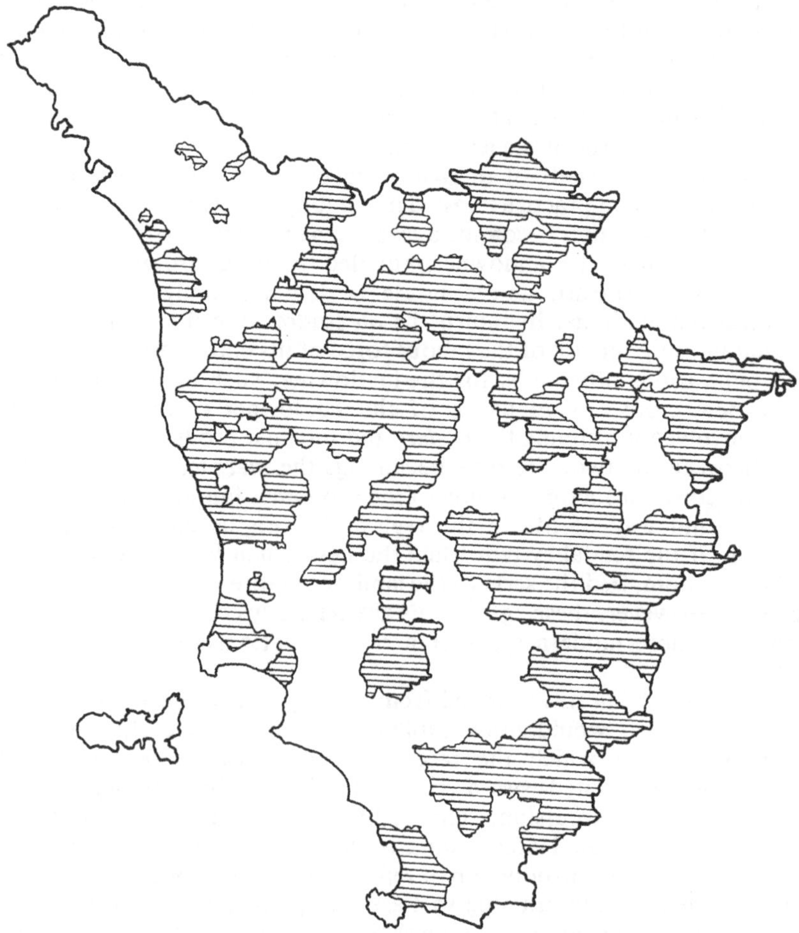

Figure 3.1 Mezzadria in Tuscany
The shading shows communal areas in which share cropping is prevalent

(After G. Beccatini (ed) 1975, reformulated by the author)

By means of the *fattoria/poderi* system the *mezzadria* became established and reproduced itself, despite the anachronism of its pre-capitalist forms, not so much for reasons of production, but as an instrument of economic and social control (Preti, 1986: 612). At the beginning of the second half of the twentieth century it still represented the predominant form of agrarian organisation in the Tuscan countryside, as Figure 3.1 shows.

It is at this point that the history of the share-cropping relationship runs into the process of diffused industrialisation that we described earlier. Indeed, the unexpected and definitive crisis of the *mezzadria* was a prerequisite of that process. The reasons behind this are not strictly economic, but also socio-cultural and territorial. We can identify four:

(1) The centre and driving force of the share-cropping structure and its self-propagation was the rural patriarchal family: an extended family which often numbered as many as 30–40 units on the larger *poderi*. An essential condition for an ideal family/*podere* relation – both for the landowner and the *mezzadro* – was that the dimensions of the latter allowed for optimal flexibility in the labour force of the family while at the same time it was able to meet all nutritional and general subsistence needs itself (Mori, 1986: 12). The main activities included the raising of livestock and, most importantly, work in the fields, although this was of an inconstant nature. During the breaks, forced or otherwise, in this work, a series of complementary jobs were undertaken, ranging from the construction of new farm buildings, to ordinary maintenance work on implements and existing buildings, the care of farmyard animals and conserving of food products, to more or less advanced levels of manufacture, turning primary products produced on the farm (wool, hides, straw, wood, etc.) into clothing and everyday articles.

The first reason, then, is the versatility of the work of which the various, or at least some, members of the share-cropping family were capable and, in particular, their familiarity with artisan-type work in producing certain articles.

(2) A characteristic feature of the share-cropping economy was, therefore, the production not only of foodstuffs, but of other articles for self-consumption. The family settled on the *podere* and isolated in the country was thus a self-sufficient microcosm. It had a rigid structure and hierarchy which revolved around the figure of the *mezzadro*, or head of the family, who disposed of the time of the other members with an authority which was derived directly from his relationship with the landowner.[13] It was the head of the family's job (often with the assistance of his elder son) to spread the cultivation correctly throughout the year; to divide the work up between male and female members of the family and according to attitudes and ability; and, finally, to make the family and farm finances work, often not an easy task. The large share-cropping family, as Bagnasco has observed, was not a commercial enterprise since its products were for self-consumption and even the landowner's portion was paid in kind; it

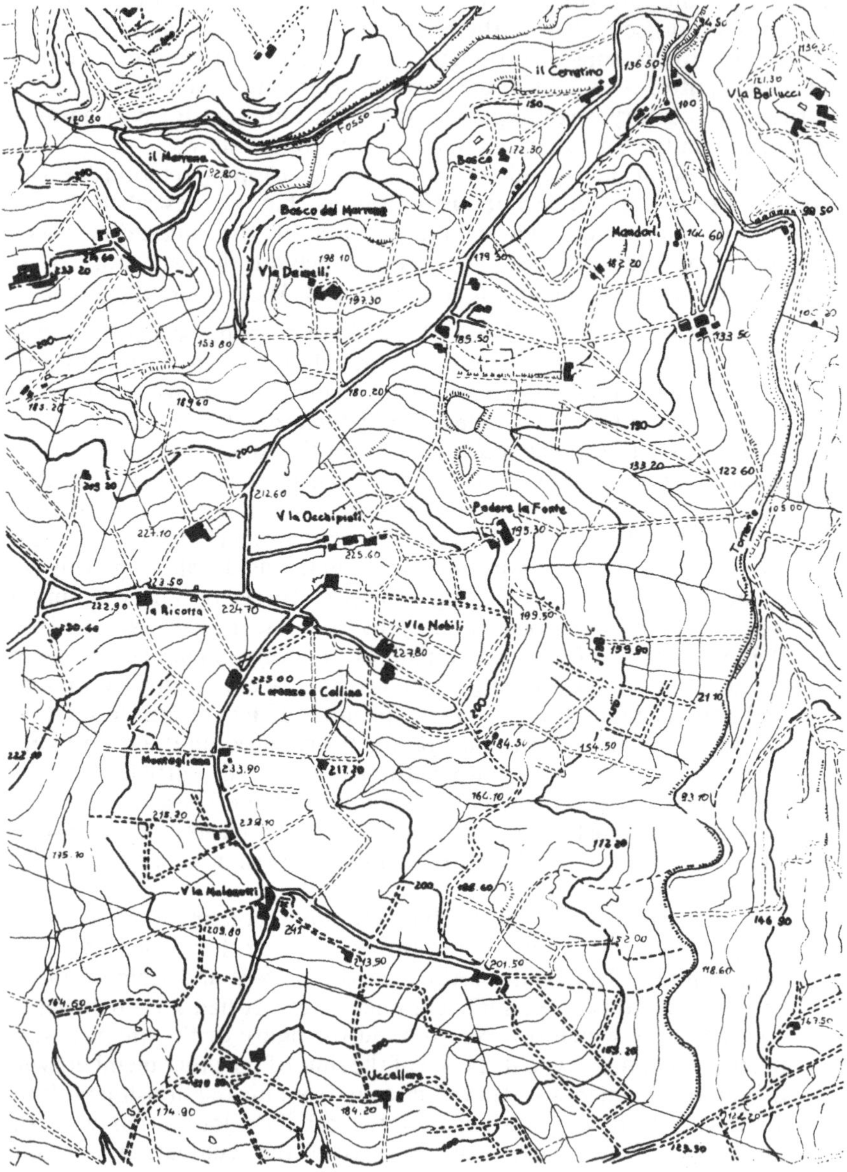

Figure 3.2 Example of the road network in the sharecropping settlement of the commune of Bagno a Ripoli

(After Amministrazione Provinciale di Firenze, 1979, reformulated by the author)

was, however, an enterprise in the sense of being a productive unit with well-defined roles and a hierarchy (Bagnasco, 1986: 746). As such it required competence and entrepreneurial skills for its management.

The second reason, then, is the set of skills of an entrepreneurial nature that the *mezzadro* and other members of the family developed.

(3) From a territorial point of view, the share-cropping farms formed a network which increased in density in the areas around the main urban centres on which their economies were based. The concentration of *mezzadri*, each with its farmhouse for the share-cropping family, was also more or less dense according to how much the land could produce. In those areas where the land was incapable of producing enough, generally in the hills and mountains, there was no share-cropping and another form of organisation grew up around a more extensive agricultural pattern. The organisation of the territory, based on scattered settlements, gave rise to a road network which connected the single farmhouses with the *fattoria*, the villages and smaller centres. This network provided share-cropping Tuscany with a very good and diffused road system, facilitating movement throughout the rural areas, as Figure 3.2 shows.

Ease of travel in the country (developed for the share-cropping system, but useful for many purposes), therefore, is a third reason.

(4) The isolated, mainly single-family, farmhouses were the basic units in this organisation of the land. As we have seen, they were the centre of life and activity. The farmhouses were the product of a continual process of growth and transformation of buildings to meet changing housing requirements of the share-croppers and production needs of the farm itself. Their function tended to determine the form, although this was sometimes affected or even determined by the urban aesthetic and architectural tendencies of the owner. The necessity of satisfying all the family's needs from the *podere* meant that a mixed pattern of cultivation was adopted.[14] Inside the house a separate section was reserved for each activity as a store after the harvest, or for processing and storing preserved products. Furthermore, there was space to shelter livestock and farmyard animals, and to store agricultural instruments. The Tuscan farmhouse, of which Figure 3.3 reproduces an example, was thus characterised by a large area of covered space.

This availability of space which, with changes in the conditions that gave rise to it, could be put to various uses, is the fourth point.

To sum up, the features inherent in the share-cropping structure which led to the development of diffused industrialisation were versatility, familiarity with artisan work, and entrepreneurial skills, on the human side, plus the existence of an excellent road network in rural areas and the abundance of space in the farmhouses, on the territorial–spatial side.

The second prerequisite for the process of diffused industrialisation and the new territorial formation derived from it is provided, as we mentioned earlier, by the tradition of artisan work in the region. The artisan tradition in

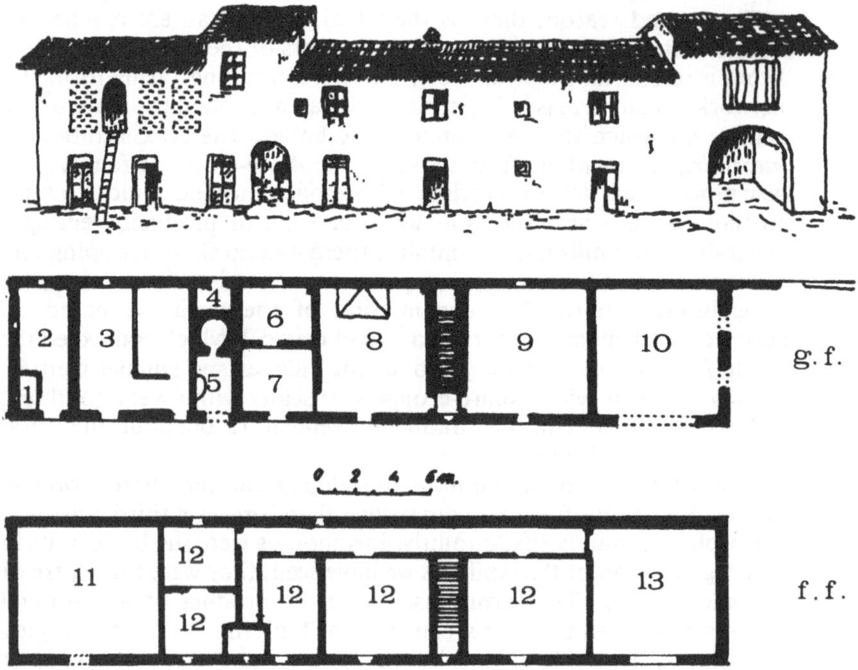

1 piggery
2 chaff cutting–room
3 cow–shed
4 hen–house
5 bake–room
6 wine–cellar
7 storeroom
8 kitchen
9 living–room
10 cart–shed
11 hay–loft
12 bed–room
13 granary

Figure 3.3 Farmhouse in the Commune of Sesto Fiorentino

(After R. Biasutti, 1938, reformulated by the author)

Tuscany has ancient roots and it was an essential component of the strong sense of autonomy and local identity of many of the larger or smaller urban centres and nuclei of the region. In the first half of this century the density of artisan activity in these areas gave rise to larger poles or zones with particular specialisations, although still within the limits of the traditional production (Becattini *et al.*, 1983: 51). In some cases the artisan structure evolved towards more particularised and advanced forms, although always maintaining, with some rare exceptions, its small size.

The organisation of the artisan workshop reproduced patterns very similar to those of the share-cropping enterprise, with the participation of the entire family in the work. However, their urban context, in comparison to the isolated rural house, led to more intense interpersonal relations, increasing the possibility of social exchange and mobility. Over time, this favoured the spread of technical knowledge connected with the different crafts, and led to the direct or indirect involvement of large parts of the population in the production or marketing of articles. This process laid the basis for the consolidation over the following decades of what was to be known under different names as 'manufacturing socialisation', 'industrial atmosphere', 'industrial environment', or 'local sub-culture'.[15] These terms all attempt to indicate, with the emphasis on different aspects, the entire economic, social and cultural predisposition of a given area to reproduce an industrial fabric composed primarily of the small enterprise that had become the cornerstone of its productive world and its social organisation.

A characteristic feature of this artisan structure and all-important for the subsequent development of diffused manufacturing activity was the elevated quota of production destined for export. The linking of a production system scattered about a complicated network of minor centres with the international market was made possible by numerous trading intermediaries who exploited the situation offered by an elite international tourism which considered Florence, Pisa, Sienna and other Tuscan cities to be not only centres of artistic heritage, but famous for the quality of their local craftwork. Among these intermediaries were the typically Florentine figures of the 'buyers'. From the beginning of the century they dealt with large commercial chains, mainly North American, seeking out in the various areas the articles particularly in demand on those markets, often developing a direct interest in a whole series of initiatives to direct, finance and improve the production in which they were interested each time.[16]

Among these initiatives, the manufacture of articles in straw, which developed in the Florentine area from the beginning of the nineteenth century, was important in the past and is particularly interesting for us as a significant example of diffused manufacturing for export.[17] This sector fully exploited the potential of the very low cost labour scattered around the share-cropping zones right from the beginning, thus anticipating a relationship between work at home in the rural areas and the production of typical goods which we will find again later, more widespread and better co-ordinated, in the organisation of much of the typical production in the area. An emblematic figure in this context was the *fattorino* (errand man), a sort of entrepreneur without a factory, who organised this work cycle, carrying out a series of operations outside manufacturing in a strict sense: he bought the raw materials where they were produced, distributed them among the *trecciaiole* (plaiters) - home workers from rural families living in villages or farmhouses - picked up the finished product and supervised its entry on to both the local and international markets. The *fattorino* is the forerunner of similar key figures in the development of much typical manufacturing, not least among them the *impannatore* (weaver) of Prato, who has carried out very similar functions in the textile production cycle.

In conclusion, the structure of the Tuscan artisan sector also contained, like the share-cropping one, considerable and specific potential: a territorial distribution based on a dense network of minor centres, a general predisposition to manufacturing work, a solid tradition of commercial relations with foreign countries and, finally, the presence of specific sectors structured around productive cycles scattered over the region.

Rural areas and diffused industrialisation

Around the middle of this century a number of elements combined to overwhelm once and for all the equilibrium which had survived up until that time in the rural world.[18] Between the second half of the fifties and the end of the sixties more than 400,000 *mezzadri* and members of their families, usually the younger ones, left their fields. This represented an enormous number for an area with a population of only 3 million. This phenomenon would have led, as it did in the South, to a mass exodus from Tuscany (Becattini (ed.), 1975: 58) had it not been for the fact that, parallel to a progressive intensification of exchange on world markets, there was a very marked increase in demand both nationally and internationally for the type of products traditionally produced in Tuscany. The resulting expansion in the production of these goods was subordinated to the containment of production costs, mainly of labour, to keep within the bounds permitted by international competition.

The abundance of labour from an agricultural background, with the particular characteristics we have already mentioned, was well-suited to this context. With regard to wages and profit in general, and adaptability to different roles and tasks, they were well-suited and willing to enter this new world of production. Their involvement in the expanding craft and industrial sectors meant that while migration did take place, it was largely restricted to short-range movement within the region (in contrast with migratory patterns in most of the rest of Italy during those years). Migration, apart from that directed towards the bigger industrial and tertiary centres, was divided between movement towards the quickly expanding manufacturing regions and the villages and units in the valleys closest to the migrators' point of origin. While the latter destinations did not offer employment opportunities, the workers could comfortably commute from them to the closest work places. There were the added advantages of cutting accommodation and general living costs and maintaining close ties with the rest of the family who may have remained on the *podere*. Subsequently, the concentration of a low-cost work force in these settlements led to the decentralisation of activities from the larger centres, the proliferation of small businesses and the rapid expansion of the original production areas (*ibid.*, p. 169).

These areas developed as 'system-areas' or 'industrial districts' (we outlined their specific characteristics earlier), by means of a series of spatial–temporal transitions: the starting point was generally an original nucleus of artisan and/or industrial activity, characterised by a high number of small companies and specialised production in one of the sectors typical of Tuscan industry from which, by means of the mechanisms mentioned above, development spread more or less gradually to the surrounding areas to form a system of centres connected by a series of interrelated functions.

These areas, dissimilar in economic strength and the level of evolution of their manufacturing structures, were situated one after the other in the valley of the Arno river and in some lateral valleys, sometimes overlapping to create areas with more than one specialisation. As Figure 3.4 shows, the Valdichiana specialised in furniture-making, the contiguous areas of the Valdarno Aretino in footwear, tanning and leather work, clothing, and goldsmithery; while to the west of Florence the textile industry flourished at Prato, the richest and most advanced productive area in Tuscany. The Valdelsa was divided between furniture-making in the upper valley, and clothing and glass in the lower part; the lower Valdarno had a mixture of tanning and footwear, the latter extending as far as Valdinievole to the west and the areas around Lucca to the east; finally, there was the furniture making area of Cascina, beyond which extended the coastal area, with an entirely different economic and territorial structure based on tourism and some large heavy industry.

Together, these areas, and all the inter-connected territories, with the exception of urban areas such as Florence, make up that territorial, and social and economic formation which for the last fifteen years or so has been considered as 'urbanised countryside', according to Becattini's definition. Figure 3.5 shows the borders, together with those of the other areas of Tuscany as they were in the mid seventies. This 'urbanised countryside', with its sometimes sparse, sometimes dense texture, dotted with roads, houses and factories, and its mixture of urban and rural, is thus the territorial image of light industry (*ibid.*, p. 181), of that process of diffusion of the manufacturing activity typical of rural, share-cropping Tuscany, from which parts of the original structures were absorbed and adapted.

The concentration of population and activities in these areas and the new dynamics of the labour market produced some profound, but diverse, effects in country areas. Many *podere* were abandoned, particularly in the more inconvenient mountain and hill country and in those areas of lowland subject to strong pressure for alternative use; while on many of those situated closer to centres of production the original families, or some members of them, stayed in the farmhouse, often changing their status by buying or renting the *podere* under the rights established by the law which abolished the *mezzadria*. The situation on the *podere* changed drastically.

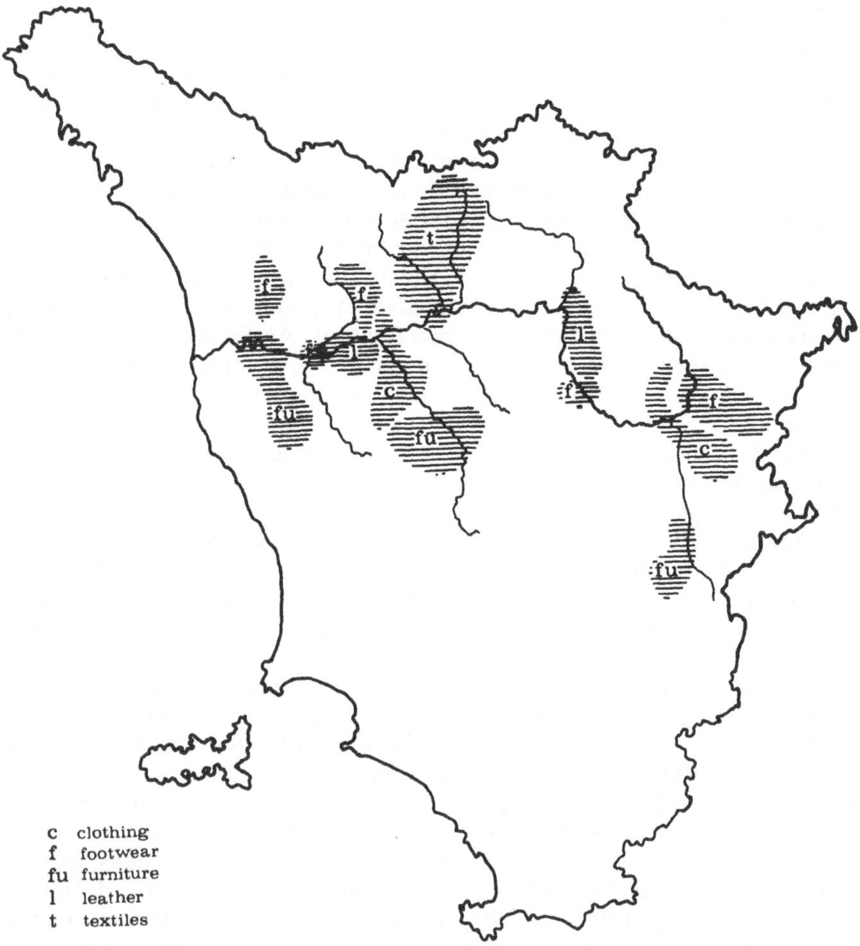

Figure 3.4 Areas of Typical Tuscan Industry

(After Irpet, 1980, reformulated by the author)

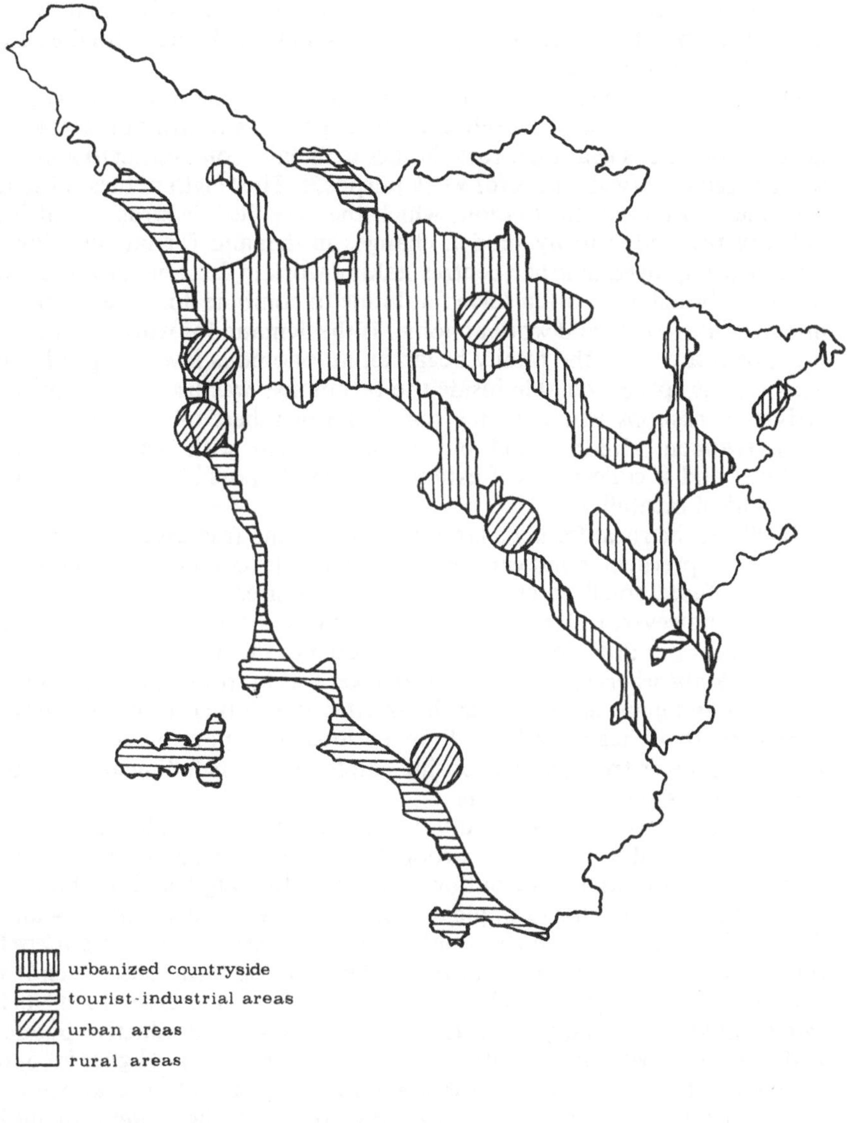

Figure 3.5 Typological areas of Tuscany

(After G. Becattini (ed) 1975, reformulated by the author)

The share-cropping family entirely employed in running the farm was replaced by a variety of combinations in which the only constant factors were the tendency for older persons to remain and the progressive limitation of agricultural practices to those requiring a minimum of labour with the aim of producing exclusively for self-sufficiency.

Of the younger members of the family, the men either moved away to the city and work, dependent or self-employed, or chose to work in factories or artisan workshops near their rural homes with daily commuting to and from work or temporary absences for work purposes. The length of these absences depended on market fluctuation, which the very flexible structure of local industry responded to by sudden changes in demand for labour. Women were also employed in urban centres, taking work in factories or the tertiary sector, although they often stayed at home to combine domestic work with opportunities to do paid work at home. If the demand for work at home was high, or if a part of the family began an autonomous low-cost production activity, the space available inside the farmhouse was used to set up small artisan workshops where all the remaining members of the family could work (women, children and old people), often with accelerated work rhythms and a collective self-exploitation made possible by a continuing hierarchical mentality.

In effect, the rural family's labour force became fractured so as to adapt itself to the precarious and variable work available, coming to form the basis of the diffused small enterprise system in the area. The family structure survived, however, to reproduce the labour force at a low cost for industry and to carry out different functions according to the moment. It functioned as a shock absorber when the labour market was in trouble, re-absorbing its members and guaranteeing them the satisfaction of their primary needs - a roof over their heads and food; in periods of expansion it allowed its members greater freedom in choosing employment, including autonomous, small business ventures at home.

The family income became very diversified, with a prevalence of income from non-agricultural sources. Production for self-consumption continued to make a substantial contribution to the family budget and to employ, if only at peak times - for example during the grape or olive harvest - all the family's labour power, which would guarantee its presence on the *podere* for these jobs. The continued use of the *podere* and the farmhouse, even if for residence or non-agricultural production, led in some cases to its being restructured, particularly in rural areas with the most productive potential and where competition with other uses was not too strong. Higher incomes, together with improved business skills acquired outside the agricultural sector sometimes led to an increased investment in the *podere*, including buying machinery, reorganising the land, and planting new crops (Orlando, 1983: 142). All this without jeopardising the main activity carried on outside the *podere*. Agriculture can no longer be considered an autonomous activity in these areas. The time devoted to agriculture and the methods used are conditioned by, and can only be understood with reference to, the overall socio-economic and territorial system which operates in the 'urbanised countryside' (Becattini *et al.*, 1983: 63).

The process of the diffusion of manufacturing activities in rural areas described above is common to all land in the 'urbanised countryside'. The working schedules of the various products give rise to a variety of situations in technical or managerial terms which affect the organisation of decentralised work and the territorial structure in general.[19] Broadly speaking, the ways in which rural labour has been involved in the industries typical of Tuscany have remained constant up to the present day. The areas of production and their relative specialisations have also remained more or less the same. However, some important changes have occurred within the development process affecting the nodal points of the production system. Reorganisation has brought technological and commercial innovations and expanded service activities. These changes are connected to the general processes of change common to national and international production systems.

All this, while affecting the various areas in different ways, seems to have affected the management of those phases of product cycle which come before and after the production process in a strict sense, where the system of small industries based on work at home and territorially diffused continues (Cavalieri, 1988: 23). Hence, the territorial coordinates fixed in the seventies have changed. As Figure 3.6 shows, the Florentine urban area has invaded the 'urbanised countryside' to the west, merging with the textile industry at Prato and other smaller centres to give rise to a polycentric metropolitan area characterised by dense settlement and a concentration of advanced functions.[20]

On the other hand, the 'urbanised countryside' is rapidly spreading over many of the lateral valleys in the Arno basin and beyond, to areas previously untouched by this type of development. What remains of the rural population in these areas is becoming involved in the same intermingling of manufacturing and agricultural activities in what has become a constant in the context of Tuscany. Indeed, this intermingling is being made more complex by new aspects deriving from changes in attitude towards the city and its contradictions. The city's growing environmental problems make living in the country an increasiangly popular alternative. Tuscan farmhouses, so well-known for the high quality of their architecture and the beauty of the surrounding landscape, are subject to an increasing amount of pressure by city dwellers wanting to buy them. Thus in many areas the social make-up of the population is changing and with it the type of occupation connected with country living. New activities are emerging based on new technology which allow a diffusion in the territory without boundaries.

Conclusion

The chief aim of this chapter has been to make clear the close and long-standing ties that exist between share-cropping in Tuscany and the 'urbanised countryside'. This continuity is evident in various aspects: the organisation of work, and the specific qualities and attitudes of the productive classes of rural origin on the one hand, and the spatial

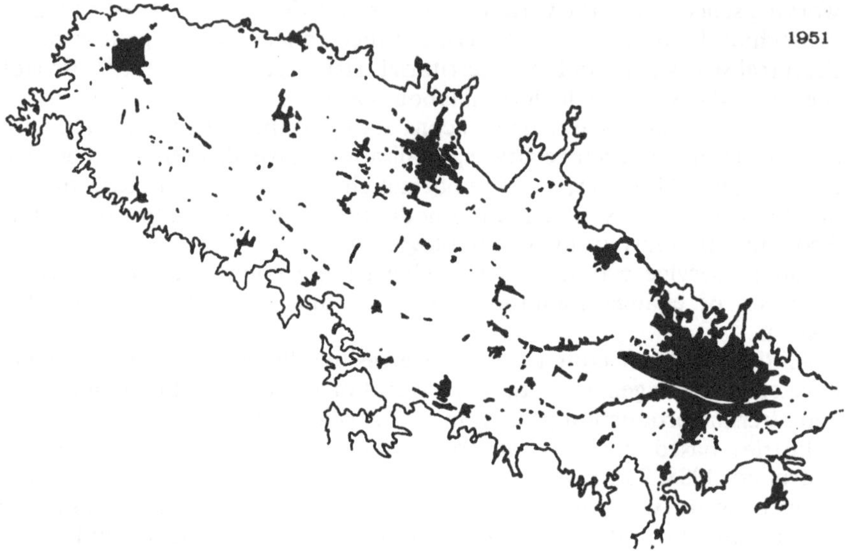

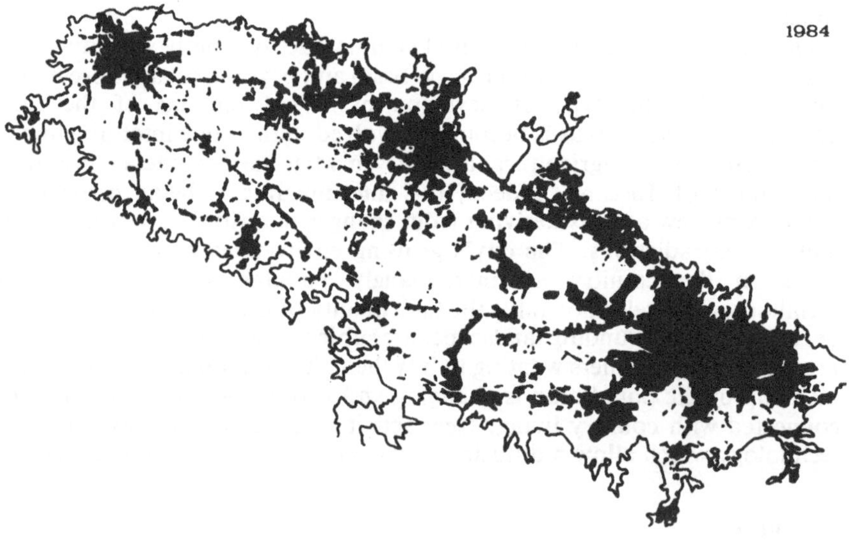

Figure 3.6 Built-up areas in the Florentine metropolitan area

(After M. Summer *et al.*, 1984, reformulated by the author)

organisation of agricultural production and the network of minor centres with an artisan tradition on the other. These are all elements which reappear, adapted to the new economic and territorial system formed in Tuscany during the sixties and seventies and, with some quite significant variations and differences, in other regions of the *Terza Italia*. These elements, which seem very specific and historically determined, have attracted relatively little attention at a time when the model of the *Terza Italia* has been upheld as a possible alternative to the crisis in mass production in the industrialised West.

Attention has been concentrated on portraying the mechanisms of an established production system, highlighting the distinctive elements considered positive and necessary for its success (see, for example, the works of Piore and Sabel cited in note 1). On the other hand, superficial treatment has been given to the negative elements, for example in terms of company and industrial relations.[21] Without wishing to undervalue the importance of some specific external factors highlighted by such studies, this chapter has emphasised the neglected, but fundamental, importance of internal historical conditions to the contemporary role of small-scale enterprise in the *Terza Italia*.

Some further considerations can be added on the basis of recent developments. Alongside the elements of stability there are signs of great change. In various regional contexts the 'urbanised countryside' seems to be establishing itself in its essential components - the diffusion of small manufacturing activities and their intermingling with agricultural activities - with some variation in the terms of interrelation between agriculture and industry. However, its borders tend to recede where the tertiary city is expanding and to advance into predominantly agricultural areas.

On a national scale the role of the *Terza Italia* is changing. Some very recent figures are revealing: in the 1980 list of Italian provinces by per capita income, three of the top five belonged to the region of Emilia Romagna, with Modena in first place; in 1990 only one of these is still present while three are from Lombardy, with Milan in first place.[22] The regions of the *Terza Italia*, with Emilia Romagna in first place, were central to the recovery and newfound expansion of the national productive apparatus, which was experiencing serious problems caused by the decline of the large factory and mass production. The *Terza Italia* was the force behind the success of Italian industry abroad.

In recent years the same regions have consolidated their production base in those specialised sectors which still represent a substantial quota of national production. It appears, however, that their strategic function is over since the northern areas of the country, with Milan and Lombardy in the lead, seem to have completed a process of restructuring which has seen, on the one hand, the large manufacturing companies (increasingly tertiarised) retake the lead in the industrial field and, on the other, the success of new advanced tertiary activities as a new strategic element in what can now be defined as a post-industrial economy. Given these changed conditions, common throughout the Western world, it is worthwhile asking whether, for whom, and on what terms, the *Terza Italia* can still be considered a valid model of industrialisation.

Notes

1. Among the first enthusiastic supporters to write about the model of the *Terza Italia* at an international level were Sabel and Piore. Cf. Sabel, C. (1982); Piore, M. and Sabel, C. (1983); Piore, M. and Sabel, C. (1984).
2. As well as North/South this dualistic viewpoint included other contrasting pairs, such as developed/underdeveloped, city/country, industry/agriculture, coast/mountain. These generally corresponded to population shifts from the 'negative' pole to the 'positive' one.
3. Lombardy and, to a lesser extent, Piedmont had been magnets during the fifties of a first strong wave of migration from nearby Veneto, a region in the north-west with a large rural hinterland.
4. The desertion of country areas was a phenomenon which, in the more general process of urbanisation, also affected regions in the north-west in direct proportion to the rural area's distance from large industrial centres and low income from agricultural activity. For Piedmont, for example, cf. Dematteis, G. (1973) p130.
5. The term *città fabbrica*, widely used at that time, was introduced at the end of the sixties by a group of aware and radical critics of mass production and its implications at a territorial and urban level. Cf. Magnaghi, A. *et al.* (1970).
6. According to some estimates oil made up 80 per cent of the entire consumption of primary energy in Italy, the highest among Western countries. Cf. Pobielski, G. (1975) p231.
7. Studies regarding the problems associated with decentralising production and the numerous others deriving from it have been the object of many attempts at reorganising and cataloguing. Among which, cf. Menghini, F. (1983); Innocenti, R., Paloscia, R. and Persia, I. (1985); Bellandi, M. (1989).
8. Cf. Bagnasco, A. (1977). The existence of a third peripheral area in contrast to the central north-west area, and the marginal south, had already been demonstrated in Bagnasco, A. and Messori, M. (1975).
9. In 1971 Tuscany alone was responsible for more than 25 per cent of the national export to the USA, and Emilia Romagna for 11 per cent of that to West Germany. Cf. Bagnasco, A., *op. cit.*, p165.
10. Cf. Garofoli, G. (1981) pp396–7. Other more or less equivalent expressions have been introduced to indicate the productive areas of the *Terza Italia*. Becattini's recycling of Alfred Marshall's term 'industrial district' is of particular interest among these: it seems to adapt itself to a number of productive situations, particularly to those in which a high number of external economies have been created in relation both to the productive sector and the area as a whole. Cf. Becattini, G. (ed.) (1979).
11. Cf. Becattini, G. (ed.) (1975). This study represents the first

comprehensive analysis of the socio-economic features of a regional economy based on diffused industrialisation and the prerequisites which made it possible; it is therefore an essential reference point for what will be said in the following paragraphs. An earlier study by IRPET (Istituto per la Programmazione Economica della Toscana) at the end of the sixties had already advanced some of the themes which became important during the seventies. Cf. IRPET (1969).

12. The contract regarding the *mezzadria* was removed from the Italian judicial statues with Law No. 756 of 1964.
13. The landowner was free to interfere in the private life of the sharecropping family if a variation in the numbers of manpower on the *podere* seemed necessary or dangerous: marriages were forced or prevented if an increase or decrease in manpower, even in the future, was thought necessary. Cf. Sereni, E. (1984) p180.
14. Mixed cultivation, with terracing and the spatial and visual relation between cultivated areas, wooded areas and scattered settlements, formed the basis of the distinctive and very high aesthetic qualities of the Tuscan landscape.
15. References to and detailed descriptions of these concepts are to be found respectively in Calza Bini, P. (1976); Becattini, G. (ed.) (1979); Bianchi, G. (1982); Trigilia, C. (1986).
16. For an analysis of the phenomenon of 'buyers', cf. Cavalieri, A. (1980).
17. A careful historical-economic analysis of the straw manufacturing sector in Tuscany and its relations with the sharecropping world is contained in Pescarolo, A. and Ravenni, G. B. (forthcoming).
18. Briefly these elements were: experience in the partisan movement in the Tuscan countryside, in which so many sharecroppers took part: frustration resulting from the fact that they never managed – when the Republic was formed – to become the owners of the land; the spread of new cultural models which were irreconcilable with the outmoded sharecropping relation and the hierarchy of the family on which it depended; and the indisputable backwardness of the *mezzadria* system.
19. The tanning of hides, for example, has, for the rapidity of its consecutive phases, stronger spatial and temporal limits than other sectors; this leads to a lot of small and integrated plants and proportionally less use of domestic labour. Cf. Furia, P. and Paloscia, R. (1981).
20. A similar phenomenon, but with less accentuated connotations, occurred in the Pisa–Livorno–Pontedera triangle. The new functions concentrated in the urban areas reorganising the system of diffused industrialisation and the management of its relations with the outside, thus restoring, in a renewed tradition of urban/rural relations, a role Florence has played at other moments in history.
21. Remarks of this sort appear in a careful critical survey of Sabel's position contained in Amin, A. (1989). Cf. also Murray, F. (1987).
22. If we consider the first 15 provinces, in 1980 seven were in Emilia and

five in Lombardy; in 1990 they were, respectively, two and eight. These figures were produced by the Camera di Commercio Industria Agricoltura e Artigianato and published in the daily newspaper *La Repubblica*, 15/7/1990.

References

Amin, A. (1989) Flexible Specialisation and Small Firms in Italy: Myths and Realities, *Antipode* Vol. 21, no. 1.

Amministrazione Provinciale di Firenze (1979) *Carta del territorio provinciale*, Firenze.

Bagnasco, A. (1977) *Tre Italie. La problematica territoriale dello sviluppo italiano*. Bologna, Il Mulino.

Bagnasco, A. (1986) Le classi e la formazione regionale, in Mori, G. (ed) *La Toscana. Storia d'Italia. Le regioni dall'Unità a oggi*. Torino, Einaudi.

Bagnasco, A. and Messori, M. (1975) *Tendenze dell'economia periferica*. Torino, Editoriale Valentino.

Becattini, G. (ed) (1975) *Lo sviluppo economico della Toscana, con particolare riferimento all'industrializzazione leggera*. Firenze, IRPET, Guaraldi.

Becattini, G. (ed) (1979) Dal 'settore industriale' al 'distretto industriale'. Alcune considerazioni sull'unità d'indagine dell'economia industriale, *L'industria*, no. 1.

Becattini, G., Bellandi, M. and Falorni, A. (1983) L'industrializzazione diffusa in Toscana: aspetti economici, in Fuà, G. and Zacchia, C. (eds) *Industrializzazione senza fratture*. Bologna, Il Mulino.

Bellandi, M. (1989) Appendice: rassegna bibliografica sui modelli di sviluppo locale, in Becattini, G. (ed) *Modelli locali di sviluppo*. Bologna, Il Mulino.

Bianchi, G. (1982) Un nuovo strumento: le matrici regionali, in Bianchi, G. (ed) *Matrici intersettoriali dell'economia regionale e programmazione*. Firenze, IRPET.

Biasutti, R. (1938) *La casa rurale in Toscana*. Bologna, Forni.

Calza Bini, P. (1976) *Economia periferica e classi sociali*. Napoli, Liguori.

Cavalieri, A. (ed.) (1980) *Il buyer in Toscana. Contributi allo studio dell'intermediazione mercantile*. Firenze, IRPET.

Cavalieri, A. (1988) Una possibile chiave di lettura delle modifiche intervenute nei meccanismi del modello toscano, in Cavalieri, A. *et al. Verso una riflessione sul modello toscano di sviluppo*. Firenze, Istituto Gramsci Toscano.

Dematteis, G. (1973) Città e campagna in Piemonte, in Mainardi, R. (ed) *Città e regione in Europa. Saggi ed analisi dei sistemi territoriali*. Milano, Angeli.

Furia, P. and Paloscia, R. (1981) Struttura produttiva e rapporti tra imprese: il caso del Valdarno inferiore, *Sociologia del lavoro*, no. 13.

Garofoli, G. (1981) Lo sviluppo delle aree periferiche nell'economia italiana degli anni Settanta, *L'industria*, no. 3.

Innocenti, R., Paloscia, R. and Persia, I. (1985) Appendice bibliografica, in Innocenti, R. (ed) *Piccola città e piccola impresa*. Milano, Angeli.

IRPET (1969) *Lo sviluppo della Toscana: un'ipotesi di lavoro*. Firenze, IRPET.

IRPET (1980) *Nuovi contributi allo studio dello sviluppo economico toscano*. Firenze, IRPET.

Magnaghi, A. *et al.* (1970) *La città-fabbrica*. Milano, Clup.

Menghini, F. (1983) Appendice bibliografica, in Fuà, G. and Zacchia, C. (eds) *Industrializzazione senza fratture*. Bologna, Il Mulino.

Mori, G. (1986) Dall'Unità alla guerra: aggregazione e disgregazione di un'area regionale, in Mori, G. (ed) *La Toscana. Storia d'italia dall'Unità oggi*. Torino, Einaudi.

Murray, F. (1987) Flexible Specialisation in the Third Italy, *Capital and Class*, no. 33.

Orlando, G. (1983) L'impatto sull'agricoltura visto da un economista agrario, in Fuà, G. and Zacchia, C. (eds) *Industrializzazione senza fratture*. Bologna, Il Mulino.

Pescarolo, A., Ravenni, G. B. (forthcoming) *Il proletariato invisibile. La manifattura del cappello di paglia nella Toscana mezzadrile 1820–1950*. Milano, Angeli.

Piore, M. and Sabel, C. (1983) Italian small business development: lessons for U.S. industrial policy, in Zisman, J. and Tyson, L. (eds) *American Industry in International Competition: Government Policies and Corporate Strategies*. Ithaca, Cornell University Press.

Piore, M. and Sabel, C. (1984) *The Second Industrial Divide: Possibilities for Prosperity*. New York, Basic Books.

Pobielski, G. (1975) *Storia dell'economia italiana 1945–1974*. Bari, Laterza.

Preti, D. (1986) Tra crisi e dirigismo; l'economia toscana nel periodo fascista, in Mori, G. (ed), *La Toscana. Storia de'Italia dall'Unità oggi*. Torino, Einaudi.

Sabel, C. (1982) *Work and politics*. Cambridge, Cambridge University Press.

Sereni, E. (1984) *Storia del paesaggio agrario italiano*. Bari, Laterza.

Summer, M. *et al.* (eds) (1984) *Processo di urbanizzazione nell'area Firenze-Prato-Pistoia*. Firenze, La casa Usher.

Trigilia, C. (1986) *Grandi partiti e piccole imprese*. Bologna, Il Mulino.

CHAPTER 4

Small-Scale Brewing and Rural Livelihoods: The Case of chicha *in Bolivia*

Colin Sage

Petty production in developing societies

Until recently much of the literature addressing the question of social and economic change in rural areas of the developing world was marked by the influence of illustrating either the persistence or decomposition of peasant households. The first, broadly 'Chayanovian', approach emphasises the adaptive capacity and internal dynamics of a household's ability to survive the effects of structural change, for example by exploiting the unpaid labour of family members and reducing household consumption, enabling it to resist the penetration of capitalism. The decomposition approach, in contrast, is influenced by a more 'Leninist' concern with explaining the socio-economic trajectory of small-scale agricultural production as a result of increased market competition. This results in the differentiation of small producers, leading eventually to the formation of a small entrepreneurial landowning class and a growing rural proletariat dependent for its survival on the sale of its labour power (Long, 1984).

While both perspectives have strong historical traditions and are equally preoccupied with explaining processes of change in developing rural societies, both have begun to experience profound limitations to concrete application. For example, the persistence or 'peasantisation' approach fails to give sufficient attention to the broader structural transformations occurring in the economy and the process of technical change in agriculture, and presents a far too homogeneous view of rural society. The decomposition approach, on the other hand, while emphasising the historical process of capitalist expansion nevertheless tends to view existing household production as if it were merely a 'blocked' stage, and doomed to eventual extinction, within a linear transition towards an economy becoming fully capitalist (Long, 1984). Moreover, it tends towards an emphasis on the primacy of off-farm labour and the role that wages perform within household reproduction. Thus, given these limitations, there is growing recognition that the application of universalistic deductive theories, with their singular logic and preconceived social and economic categories, no longer adequately reflect empirical diversity, especially in the wide variations in agrarian systems, household morphology and the resilience of forms of small-scale production (Buttel and Goodman, 1989). Such criticism is part of a current re-evaluation of the impasse in development studies (Booth, 1985; Vandergeest and Buttel, 1988).

As an example of the above one can refer to studies of the Andean countryside which have documented the vital contribution of rural labour to capitalist accumulation, whether employed by large-scale agricultural units, the mining industry or urban-based enterprises (Long and Roberts, 1978, 1984; Mallon, 1983; Figueroa, 1982). Besides permanent outmigration from rural communities, periodic involvement in wage work, though varying by frequency and duration, can be interpreted as evidence of a process of decomposition amongst the peasantry. Yet while the sale of labour power amongst both men and women may, in some localities, be central to the reproduction of rural households, most units survive the effects of structural change introduced by new social relations through generating a portfolio of strategies. Besides occasional or sustained wage employment, these can include the provision of use values, the production of agricultural commodities for the market, and involvement in a variety of petty trading and artisanal activities. The development of a repertoire of activities by individual households offers the opportunity to generate even small amounts of cash income to meet consumption requirements, especially in the absence of collective welfare provision and a limited market in wage labour.

One approach that has sought to find a way out of the apparent dilemma between peasant persistence or decomposition has emphasised the role and importance of small-scale enterprises engaged in petty commodity production within developing capitalist social formations. This means, first, beginning from a perspective where so-called peripheral economies are considered as generalised commodity economies and not 'pre-capitalist', 'traditional' or 'peasant' societies located on the margins of capitalist markets and economic forces (Long, 1986). Secondly, small-scale enterprises themselves are not to be seen as intrinsically transitional and prone to imminent demise, nor as self-perpetuating units untouched by economic forces. Rather, 'they must be examined closely to establish the precise ways in which commodity exchange and market mechanisms shape and reproduce these specific forms of production' (Long *et al.*, 1986, p. 2). The commoditisation approach thus seeks to explain the ways by which rural households become increasingly reliant on transactions conducted through the market, both as producers of agricultural produce and other commodities, including labour power, and as purchasers of necessary consumption goods and renewal of means of production (Friedmann, 1980; Scott, 1986).

While the analysis of small-scale household enterprises engaged in petty commodity production represents a significant advance on the persistence–decomposition debate, there remain important areas for further attention. One, for example, concerns the social relations within household enterprises. Here, feminist analysis has alerted us to the dangers of treating the household as a 'black box' within which one could assume a mutuality of interests and harmony of objectives. Rather, we know that gender and age are the principal parameters which determine an internal division of labour and the distribution of rewards, and these must form part of the analytical tools with which we unlock the concept of household.

A second area requiring more detailed attention concerns the way in which household enterprises are treated within a wider (local and regional) context. This involves, for example, giving importance to the household's construction of social networks, its relations with economically powerful individuals (merchants, landowners, truck operators, etc), and the nature of interactions with rural and other development agencies and state institutions. It has been argued that it is necessary to develop a more actor-oriented perspective that accords rural households a more dynamic, strategic role in economic change in which they actively shape and mediate external forces (Long, 1988). This perspective contrasts with the more functionalist view where the state, it is argued, promotes and harnesses petty commodity production for the purpose of capital accumulation in the urban industrial sector through cross-sectoral transfers of the agricultural surplus (de Janvry, 1981).

A social actor, or 'farmer first' (Chambers, 1983) approach, on the other hand, allows us to recover the notion of 'livelihood' to refer to the forms of production that together provide for the material and social reproduction of the household without embodying assumptions regarding the status of individual members. It accords equal weight to agricultural and non-agricultural activities, the production of commodities and use-values. The notion of livelihood is especially useful in contexts where the state is conspicuously absent and local economies are characterised by productive activities that are responses to opportunities rather than directed by planned interventions. In such contexts it could be suggested that the repertoire of household activities is designed to fulfil cultural as well as material needs. This is not to fall back upon notions of 'tradition', however, or to suggest that such activities might not contribute to accumulation, either locally or elsewhere. Rather, households develop livelihood solutions, according to their resources and aspirations, in contexts where there is no provision of welfare goods and where they collectively struggle to secure essential services.

This chaper, then, takes the notion of livelihood as a central theme in which it is possible to examine the different forms and degrees of petty commodity production in the context of different household structures. By moving beyond the conventionally ascribed boundaries of units of production in order to 'deconstruct' the household, this reveals not only internal structures and individual roles, but the contributions of different economic activities – including those hidden within the domestic sphere. The chapter describes the manufacture of maize beer (*chicha*) by women in one Andean village as an example of the important but varied roles that one activity can perform. It is illustrative to assess the function of this activity according to the composition and landholding stratum of the household, and two case-studies are briefly presented in order to do this.

The context

The case study of *chicha* production is set in the community of Santa Rosa which comprises some 62 households and is located on a hillside some 100 kms northwest of the city of Cochabamba in central Bolivia (see Figure 4.1). Despite considerable difficulties of access the majority of households in this area dedicate themselves to agricultural commodity production and have become firmly incorporated into the regional economy. Nevertheless, while agriculture remains the mainstay of the local economy, many households are involved in a range of non-agricultural, income-generating activities. Such activities may be said to have either a complementary or supplementary relationship to agriculture. By complementary it is meant that such activities serve to extend and deepen control over means of production, especially labour power which is procured through forms of debt bondage, and which offer a route towards high and sustained income generation through a combination of agricultural intensification and economic diversification. Supplementary activities, on the other hand, are necessary in order to acquire extra cash income beyond that derived from agricultural production and the sale of wage labour in order to meet the needs of household reproduction.

Indeed, the local labour market is so poorly developed due to the availability of land, wages by themselves do not offer sufficient incentive to work for others. Thus the movement of labour between households is largely compensated by a reverse flow of loans of means of production (animal traction, seed and chemical fertilisers). Nor are there many opportunities for seasonal or more permanent wage labour. The low level of capital investment in the country and the long-established dominance of small-scale enterprises within the region leave little room for migrants from the highlands. Thus, small-scale activities in Santa Rosa, while they may not attract significant additional income from outside, do stimulate the circulation of money within the community, especially for those households which might otherwise have difficulty in providing for themselves. In this respect it is important to note that, irrespective of their functional role, most of these activities are in the hands of women and include a variety of forms of petty trading, weaving and, especially, the brewing of maize beer (*chicha*).

Within the area where Santa Rosa is located, as throughout much of rural

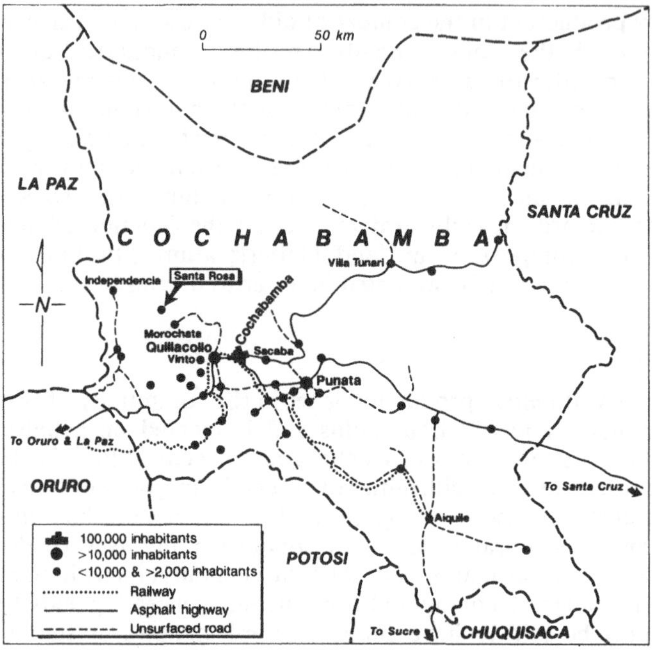
0 50 km
BENI
LA PAZ
SANTA CRUZ
C O C H A B A M B A
N
Villa Tunari
Independencia
Santa Rosa
Cochabamba
Morochata
Quillacollo
Vinto
Sacaba
Punata
To Oruro & La Paz
ORURO
To Santa Cruz
Aiquile
100,000 inhabitants
>10,000 inhabitants
<10,000 & >2,000 inhabitants
Railway
Asphalt highway
Unsurfaced road
POTOSI
To Sucre
CHUQUISACA

BRAZIL
N
SOUTH
BOLIVIA
AMERICA
PANDO
PERU
BENI
LAPAZ
COCHABAMBA
SANTA CRUZ
B O L I V I A
ORURO
Pacific
Ocean
POTOSI
CHUQUISACA
PARAGUAY
TARIJA
CHILE
ARGENTINA
0 250 km

Bolivia in general, the state plays a largely tributary role. Its nominal presence in the Ayopaya highlands serves to legitimate networks of local power exercised by merchants and truck operators in alliance with large local landowners and other members of the rural elite. These informal structures of local power have severely undermined the effective organisation of peasant syndicates and other community bodies which are largely manipulated by a few land-rich households on behalf of external actors with whom they have close ties. One example of such networks of local power is provided by the collection of the *chicha* tax, to which we will later briefly return.

Theoretical issues relating to the household

Differentiation

Conducting an analysis of small-scale household enterprises, it was argued above, requires a more subjective 'actor-oriented' perspective. This allows us to recognise the role of decision-making at the individual and household level in negotiating, for example, the balance between production for exchange and the maintenance of use-value production for direct consumption. This consequently creates the notion of the *degree* to which the reproduction cycle of the household is realised through the production and exchange of commodities. However, by recognising the importance of negotiated interactions between externally generated opportunities and constraints and individual needs, rather than determined outcomes imposed by economic forces, concrete empirical investigation is vital in revealing the values, orientations and 'life-worlds' of individual households (Long, 1989).

Greater integration of actor-oriented perspectives provides a more dynamic appreciation of the relationship between commoditised and non-commoditised spheres both within and beyond the household (Smith, 1985; Long, 1986). This is vital, as one of the distinguishing characteristics of petty commodity production is the control which is exercised over the organisation of household labour, although this is problematic as we shall see. Moreover, as domestic work and other forms of unpaid labour represent non-commoditised relations within the household, so it is possible to identify the persistence of inter- and supra-household relationships that cannot be explained by purely economic logic. Such Andean institutions as the reciprocal exchange of labour (*ayni*, *mink'a*) and products (*trueque*), or the role of fictive kin relationships (*compadrazgo*) in constructing social networks remain a vital part of rural life, although they are not static 'traditional' forms that have remained untouched by wider processes of economic change. Indeed, the use of such terms as *ayni*, conventionally applied to the reciprocal exchange of a day's labour, can disguise highly exploitative mechanisms used by land-rich households to ensure a cheap

---

Figure 4.1 Map of the Cochabamba region

supply of labour (Sànchez, 1982; Sage, 1990). It is important to be cogniscent of such mechanisms and the ways they might be used by petty commercial activities to secure non-monetary returns.

A further vital issue concerns the degree to which households are differentiated according to their control over means of production such as land, livestock, capital and labour. Such a recognition is distinct from the classical marxist view of the differentiation process resulting in an inevitable polarisation of the rural population into opposing classes, as measured by the universalisation of wage labour. To emphasise the importance of wage labour for the reproduction of poor households tends towards a forward projection of the differentiation process and may refer to petty commodity producers as wage workers using such 'sociological' categories as 'hidden', 'disguised' or 'concealed' (Goodman and Redclift, 1981). While, in some areas, off-farm employment may generate an important part of the household income, it is by no means universally the case that labour markets, or rural households, should function in this manner. Often, the restricted opportunities available to rural labour, which reflect the form and degree of capitalist development locally, may ensure that those in the poorest stratum continue to reproduce themselves from a combination of agricultural and non-agricultural activities. Thus, not only may patterns of inequality between households be obscured, but together with the high-risk circumstances of peripheral agrarian societies, such patterns are unlikely to be consolidated into an established class structure: class membership within such societies being ambiguous, insecure and changing (Long, 1986).

Lehmann (1982) also argues against an account of differentiation that leads to notions of polarised, solidary classes. The only alternative, he suggests, is to view differentiation in a variety of ways: by source and amount of income, landholding, institutional affiliations, even language and ethnicity, and above all, by sector of activity. While most households may be engaged in agriculture or animal husbandry this is far from an exclusive activity:

> . . . some engage in trade, wholesale and retail, in moneylending, and others migrate intermittently to mining centres, towns, far-off plantations and so on. Their livelihoods are achieved through a variety of mechanisms . . . (Lehmann, 1982, pp. 140–1).

Such mechanisms of diversified economic activities, often labelled 'livelihood strategies', may acquire significance for both poorer and wealthier households. Amongst the land-poor, for example, involvement in non-agricultural income-generating activities, including the sale of wage labour, may be necessary to supplement income from the sale of agricultural commodities and use-value production in order to ensure household reproduction. Amongst the land-rich, on the other hand, involvement in such commercial activities as trading, livestock dealing, transport, or non-agricultural commodity production such as brewing, may represent lucrative opportunities for income generation and saving, leading to investment and the raising of the level of the productive forces in agriculture. For this reason economic diversification may make a significant contribution to social differentiation and offers some functional complementarity with agricultural production. This underlines the need for the careful investigation of differentiation from specific empirical cases and not to assume that it can simply be read off from abstract theoretical propositions.

Gender and generation

In the preceding discussion the household has been treated as an unproblematic, internally-coherent entity, differentiated from others according to its material resources, involvement in non-agricultural activities and social aspirations, yet one where the individual and the household are treated as synonymous and indivisible. Such an assumption implies the equal distribution of consumption goods, equal access to productive resources, and subsumes the activities of individuals as mere components of a wider collective household strategy. Sufficient work has now demonstrated that it is grossly erroneous to assume a harmony of objectives in which the household is characterised by virtues of 'pooling, sharing and generosity' (Harris, 1981; Friedmann, 1986).

Feminist analysis, in particular, has emphasised the internal divisions of labour and differential distribution of the product along lines of gender, age and marital status. Other authors have explicitly questioned the status and validity of the unitary concept of 'household'. For example, in Africa the diversity of conjugal arrangements suggests that it may be necessary to identify smaller functional units (often matrifocal) which possess overlapping memberships and highly permeable boundaries (Guyer and Peters, 1987). In other words it may be erroneous to assume that a congruence of diverse familial functions operate entirely independently of other family units, and that residential boundaries coincide with functional boundaries (Oppong, 1982).

In order to illustrate these points it has been observed that as the level of commodity relations deepens within the reproductive cycle of the household, social relations may be despotically reinforced in order to control the labour power of family members (Smith, 1986). Preventing the subdivision of land and maintaining control over the labour of adult sons and daughters is a source of considerable internal conflict within households, particularly amongst those with the greatest resources. Between parents and their children there can be substantial discord over the allocation of roles and distributional rewards, and this may be accompanied by struggles between siblings over proposed divisions of family property (Long, 1977). The principal conflict, however, arises from the irreconcilable differences between the objectives of the senior generation – especially the male head of household – and the aspirations of sons and daughters.

A second major issue that must be emphasised is the tendency either to ignore the structural morphology of the household or to treat it as conforming to simple 'nuclear' or 'extended' forms. What is then posed as an interesting analytical issue is how far household structure correlates with resource endowment and in turn influences economic diversification. Naturally, few rural communities comprise a collection of ideal-typical households all exclusively dedicated to agricultural production. In Santa Rosa, for example, almost thirty per cent of households do not conform to either 'nuclear' or 'extended' forms. Indeed, within the land-poorest category (with access to less than 1.5 hectares) exactly half of the 26 households consist of those headed by women, aged couples and single males. This attests to the instability of the conventionally-viewed household as a unit of production and reproduction (Deere, 1978). As households which are neither 'nuclear' nor 'extended' are characterised above all by inadequate labour power, which severely limits their ability to produce agricultural commodities from a limited land base, their reproduction must be secured through alternative economic strategies.

However, in order to understand the role and significance of such strategies, it is necessary to establish the wider context of gender relations and how these interface with production and reproduction to determine the sexual division of labour within the household. Here it is necessary to move from the general to the specific in order to investigate the concrete circumstances of role allocation, social constraints and economic opportunities. This we shall do by drawing upon data from Santa Rosa.

As mentioned earlier, one of the over-riding features of the locality is its high degree of dedication to agricultural commodity production especially with the cultivation of potato. It is believed that the intensification of commodity production during the recent period has wrought a substantial shift in the balance of gender relations, a process that has been observed elsewhere (Bourque and Warren, 1981; see also Beneria and Sen, 1988). While the involvement of women in agricultural production varies according to landholding strata, family life cycle and household composition, women's roles have become more circumscribed, specialised and undervalued since, for example, the epoch of the hacienda.[1] Although women are allocated such tasks as sowing, with all its associations with fertility, they are rigidly excluded from ploughing. Thus, men are able to carry out all stages of the agricultural cycle, including the planting of seed when necessary, while women - even in female-headed households - are sanctioned to rely upon men for particular tasks. For those women without access to male labour and, under dominant notions of gender roles, who are prevented from participating fully in agricultural commodity production, such income-generating activities as petty trading and *chicha* production become central to their survival.

Women are, of course, responsible for the burdens of ensuring the biolgoical and material reproduction of the household. While the main concern of this chapter is with one of women's roles in the production of exchange values, it should be remembered that these go on alongside the extraordinary demands made upon women's time, energy and well-being by childbirth and lactation and the daily demands of servicing the needs of household members. In Santa Rosa, for example, a survey of women's completed fertility history revealed that the average number of births per woman was 7.88, which means that besides spending almost six years of her life in pregnancy, a woman spends a further ten years lactating (Sage, 1990).

Moreover, women play a vital role in the production of use values within the household which, besides agricultural tasks and the pasturing of livestock, include the spinning and weaving of wool to produce blankets, sacks and carrying cloths. Finally, it could be asserted that the lack of welfare provision - besides the local primary school there is no other form of state investment - has greater repercussions for the demands made upon women as caretakers of health.

Furthermore, as many women's activities are physically performed within the household, produce use values and are accorded the status of 'domestic' labour, they are often rendered invisible and unworthy of attention (Harris, 1981). Indeed, Mackintosh describes the petty selling of goods amongst women in a Senegalese village which she only gradually became aware of through living in a household. Yet she recognised that this separate sphere of exchange was very important to the way in which women succeeded in providing for their families (Mackintosh, 1988). The important lesson here is that we should approach such activities, not purely to evaluate their commodity producing status, but rather their effectiveness in meeting certain household needs (defined or not), within time and resource constraints, in ways that may not be immediately apparent.

Chicha production

Chicha (maize beer) is an alcoholic beverage whose production and use dates back to pre-Colombian times and is strongly associated with Andean rural culture. Though symbolic associations remain, today in the Cochabamba region of Bolivia *chicha* fulfils an important economic role - as a source of income for many rural households and as revenue through taxation for the regional authorities. The tax levied on *chicha* production has provided a substantial source of revenue to finance infra-structural projects and public works as well as covering part of the running costs of urban institutions. Since the early 1960s at least one third of all regional revenue has been provided by the *chicha* tax, of which one third is also taken by the National Treasury (IESE, 1975). It is evident, therefore, that the tax has proved an effective way by which the state extracts a surplus from the countryside to finance urban investment and promote industrial accumulation while doing nothing to raise the levels of agricultural production and rural living standards.

Within the Cochabamba region production largely remains rooted at the household level and under the control of women, although there is considerable diversity in the scale, frequency and style of manufacture. In many parts of the central Cochabamba Valleys, where population pressures and fragmentation severely constrain access to land, income derived from non-agricultural petty production and trading activities exceeds in importance that derived from farming. Here there is a marked concentration of *chicherias* and almost continuous production of *chicha*.[2] In the surrounding highlands, however, agriculture generally remains predominant, although occasional *chicha* production may provide an important and often vital source of income. In Santa Rosa, for example, many households produce some *chicha*, usually to celebrate a major family event such as a marriage, or the community's patron-saint day, while a few also derive substantial income from occasional elaboration. Overall, the importance of *chicha* as an economic subsystem has strong parallels with traditional brewing in many parts of Africa, which is also largely under the control of women.[3]

The procedure for producing *chicha* is a skill that is handed down from mother to daughter and, although some men may acquire the knowledge through assisting in the process, it is an activity that remains firmly under women's control and is an integral part of their repertoire of income generating activities. The process commences by turning maize into malt through soaking, sprouting, drying and milling of the kernels. The malt is then mixed with water in a cooking process that takes almost twenty-four hours, requiring careful skill and judgement and considerable labour. Although women control the entire operation, other household members are expected to help - in the collection of fuelwood, in carrying water, and in moving the liquid between containers - with older sons involved in the heavier tasks. Those women without sons or a spouse in their household usually hire labour to cut and carry fuelwood but, with the help of other kin or neighbours, manage the remainder of the operation themselves. In the Cochabamba Valleys, where production is more continuous and competitive, producers add more sugar and often cane alcohol to make their *chicha* sweeter and stronger. In Santa Rosa, on the other hand, while a small amount of sugar may be added to reduce the naturally slightly bitter flavour, the product is rather more 'authentic' and gruel-like.

It should be clear that *chicha* performs a variety of cultural and economic functions according to different groups of households at different times of the year in different local contexts. In order to illustrate more vividly the diversity of objectives with which *chicha* is associated, we can examine the circumstances in Santa Rosa between July 1981 and June 1982. During this period some 24 of the 62 resident households engaged in *chicha* production on at least one occasion. Of these some six households produced relatively small quantities of *chicha* during the time of *Carnaval* in late February to facilitate family celebrations. A further two households produced much larger quantities of *chicha* on the occasion of *Carnaval*, the festival of San Juan in June, and Republic Day on 6th August for consumption by the community as part of their obligations as *alcaldes*.[4] Finally, some 16 households engaged in the production and sale of *chicha* at least once over this period, although the frequency, function and importance of this activity varied considerably amongst this group.

For example, even for the four woman-headed households which produced *chicha* during this period this activity does not equally represent the same income-generating livelihood solution to their situation, for the frequency with which they engage in production varies from once to four times over the year. This variation reflects the existence of alternative economic opportunities and the level of need for cash, besides the more practical constraints such as the availability of maize and labour within the household.

In contrast, at least two other 'nuclear' households use *chicha* more as a means to secure labour power through indebtedness as much as for its income-generating potential. This provides them with labourers to work on their lands, freeing household members to engage in other, more lucrative non-agricultural economic activities. In these cases, women's labour is directly complementary to their partners' expressed need for cheap agricultural labour, and together this contributes to the household fulfilling the objectives of expanded accumulation through simultaneous intensification and diversification of production. This will be illustrated in a little more detail below.

Returning, however, to the frequency and timing of production: there are peaks in the availability of *chicha* which coincide with religious and secular festivals during the course of the year. At such times there are several producers offering *chicha* for sale, besides those households which produce purely for domestic consumption; although it appears that women reach an informal agreement between themselves in order to avoid the risk of over-production and being left with unsold *chicha*. If at other times a household should urgently need to generate cash then, equally, there is no reluctance in Santa Rosa to drinking outside formal occasions. Indeed, with no competition a household could be assured of selling its 350 litres of *chicha* within the space of two or three days.[5]

Yet the transaction between producers and consumers of *chicha* is complicated by the incomplete monetarisation of the local economy, and this prevents a straightforward realisation of the potential profits that can be derived from its production. While, on the one hand, this allows the land-rich, *chicha*-producing households to secure labour power in cancellation of debts accumulated from drinking sprees, on the other hand land-poor households usually have less need for labour than they do for cash. Often products are used to settle debts, usually the less valuable tubers *oca* and *lisa* rather than potatoes and maize. Several producers commented that around 25 per cent of potential earnings are lost in unrecovered debts, and that this would be higher if women producers did not visit the drinkers who owed them money to harass them for payment.

Nevertheless, most producers spoke of profit margins of up to 2,000 pesos or US$80 at 1981 prices on the average production of around 350 litres. Such profit margins are largely possible because women normally secure the 200 kgs of maize which is used in the process through barter, rather than through commercial purchase, or the use of household produced grain which is sold or consumed as food. Moreover, some women occasionally fatten a small pig on the sediment remaining from a previous round of *chicha* production, then slaughter, fry and serve this, togther with boiled maize kernals, as *chicharron*, to hungry drinkers. This may realise a further profit of around US$30. Thus, while the elaboration of *chicha* is extremely hard work for women producers, it represents a significant source of earnings for the household. It also represents, as mentioned earlier, a substantial source of revenue for the regional authorities and the national state. Before providing two brief and contrasting profiles of *chicha* producers, it is revealing to establish the parasitical structure that prospers from the extraction of surplus from such producers.

Since 1910, a succession of national legislative decrees have specified the rate of tax to be levied upon *chicha* producers and the infrastructural projects that were to benefit from the revenue. These have included the installation of a mains water system, the paving of the streets and the construction of a football stadium within the city of Cochabamba, as well as meeting part of the running costs of the local university (IESE, 1975). Yet the collection of the *chicha* tax represents a considerable difficulty for the regional authorities.

For example, in the central Cochabamba Valleys, where there is a high concentration of *chicherias* supporting an almost continuous pattern of production, the monitoring and collection of revenue is performed by the regional *chicha*-tax office. In the more remote and inaccessible parts of the region, however, the authorities use local merchants and other members of the rural elite to levy the tax. Here, the rights to collect revenue on *chicha* production in circumscribed areas are publicly auctioned every year, though in practice the bidding is a charade to disguise what has in effect become something of an historic right for certain individuals. The collector who wins the right to levy the *chicha* tax in his area pays his bid to the regional office, and this supposedly reflects the estimated volume of production locally. With this authorisation, the collector has a strong incentive to ensure that all *chicha* producers pay their tax, as it enters *his* own pocket.[6]

In Santa Rosa in 1981 each producer paid just under US$10, on each occasion that they brewed *chicha*, to the local tax collector who lives in the district capital of Morochata. Don José once owned a large hacienda in the area, which was partially expropriated under the Agrarian Reform, and now sustains his waning aristocratic pretentions from his collecion of the *chicha* tax. In Santa Rosa, as in every other large village in the area, a resident informant records the number of occasions each producer manufactures *chicha* and passes these details to Don José, in return for a small consideration, when he makes his twice-yearly visits for tax collection purposes. In this way the *chicha* tax has come to represent a form of surplus extraction from petty producers which contributes to the support of a rural elite in alliance with a bureaucratic tributary state.

Case studies of chicha producers

It was emphasised earlier that *chicha* production does not represent the same income-generating function or livelihood solution for each and every household. Rather, there is some considerable variation that reflects the material resources, social aspirations and economic strategies within diverse household forms. In an attempt to provide a flavour of these different qualitative elements, we can briefly compare the circumstances of two *chicha*-producing households.

Case study 1

Hortencia and Ramiro Valdivieso occupy an unusual position in Santa Rosa for they have the most diversified economic base of any household for the following reasons:

(1) Ramiro is an administrator of a small nearby lead mine and is the only person in the community to earn a salary.
(2) The household owns almost 3.5 hectares of land, 2.5 ha of which was initially allocated under the Agrarian Reform to the local school. Taking advantage of the lack of awareness and mobilisation amongst local people, the Valdiviesos at first illegally occupied this land, then later had the appropriate authorities approve their *de facto* ownership. This land is usually under potato production.
(3) Eight of their nine children now live in the family's second home in the city of Cochabamba and hold regular jobs, while just one son and his wife remain in the family home in Santa Rosa.
(4) Hortencia displays the sharpest commercial acumen in the area and engages in a number of income-generating activities. For example, she travels through the surrounding communities trading articles of clothing for sheep which she then resells on her next clothes buying visit to the city. During 1981–82 Hortencia sold some forty head of sheep, earning close to US$500 from these transactions. Moreover, she is the only person to trade in kerosene, which most households use in only small quantities for their primitive lamps. This may explain why she is able to exchange one litre of kerosene for one *arroba* (12 kgs) of maize, a mark-up of ten times in monetary equivalents.

Once Hortencia has acquired sufficient maize through such exchanges she then turns this into *chicha*. On each of the six occasions when she produced *chicha* during 1981–82, Hortencia made a profit in excess of US$100. This enhanced profit margin is partly explained by the quality of her *chicha* and her larger scale of operations, but also because her personality ensures that she loses considerably less than the 25 per cent of turnover in unrecovered debts of which most producers complain. Her early morning rounds to collect debts from hung-over neighbours, who often plead an absence of memory and no cash, provide her with a cheap and rapidly assembled labour-force as debtors are promptly told to report for work within the hour. Thus, besides the monetary income that is derived from the sale of *chicha*, the household is able to mobilise a temporary labour force through a form of debt-bondage which performs the full range of agricultural tasks, besides cutting and carrying the fuel wood necessary for the next round of *chicha* production. Given the high opportunity cost of Ramiro's job as mine administrator, it is economically rational that agricultural work on the Valdiviesos' land be performed by bonded labour which pays off its drinking debts as the lowest daily wage rate.

In this way the Valdivieso household has become one of the richest and most powerful in the locality. It is engaged in a highly diversified range of profitable activities in Santa Rosa while maintaining a secure economic and residential base in the city. It possesses a carefully constructed network of social relationships with economically influential actors in the area, for example landowners and merchants, through the use of *compadrazgo* (fictive kin) relations. It has access to a bonded, compliant pool of labour that not only performs work but, when selectively patronised and cultivated, is able to legitimise the Valdiviesos' authority within the public domain. Consequently, we can see that Hortencia's production of *chicha* performs truly multiple functions and is thoroughly integrated within the household's overall repertoire of activities.

Case study 2

In contrast, Doña Amelia is a woman of at least seventy years who lives with three male grandchildren. The two eldest, Ignacio and Ivan, 21 and 18 respectively, are the offspring of Amelia's only son, Fidel, who died in 1972. Fidel's widow left Santa Rosa shortly after her husband's death, leaving Amelia to care for her children. The third grandchild, Nicolàs, is eleven and the son of Amelia's second daughter and an earlier partner. Although this daughter lives with her husband and their five children in Santa Rosa, they prefer that Nicholàs remains with Amelia. Such complex kinship relations within (and between) household units are by no means exceptional and warn against assuming conventional 'nuclear' or 'extended' forms. Indeed, households with such complex internal structures may often be marked by highly individualised or ego-centred livelihood activities as opposed to more 'collective' strategies.

For example, in the case of Amelia's household Ignacio and Ivan together work one hectare of leased land on which they produce potatoes for the market, the income from which enters their own pockets and is not used to meet any household expenses. Thus, in order to provide materially for Nicholàs and herself, and to meet the food needs of all four, Amelia relies upon two tried and trusted mechanisms for securing cash income. First, Amelia produces *chicha* on four or five occasions each year, which provides an annual income of around 10,000 pesos (US$400). She supplements this by baking and selling bread rolls made with wheat flour purchased in the city, providing an additional income of 600 pesos per month. Thus Amelia exploits two relatively high-income generating activities which together meet the costs for the material reproduction of a household in which there is little use value production. However, the fragile structure and limited emotional bonding of the household, which is frequently evident in the open conflict between members, especially Ignacio and Ivan, have created two relatively independent spheres of operation.

For example, the returns from agriculture are largely invested by Ignacio and Ivan in items of personal rather than collective consumption. Amelia's non-agricultural activities, on the other hand, play a decisive role in maintaining household reproduction although they are only grudgingly supported by her two older grandchildren, who cut and transport fuelwood. Thus, the household has only a limited repertoire of activities, and these are personally pursued rather than collectively supported and sustained. However, its local kinship networks offer a bedrock of security at times of difficulty and play an important role in strategies of household survival.

Conclusions

As the case studies suggest, the circumstances which encourage women's involvement in *chicha* production are complex and wide ranging. The decision to engage in brewing is influenced by such specific factors as the form and composition of the household; its resources in land, labour and capital; the degree to which it is able to reproduce itself from alternative activities; and its wider social and economic aspirations. Yet there are also more general structural factors which influence the combination and function of women's roles and activities, such as the social construction of gender relations and the operation of labour markets within the region.

For example, it was argued earlier that the gender division of labour in Santa Rosa marginalises women's involvement in agricultural production. In households conforming to nuclear and extended compositional forms, the requirements of household production are largely met by using family, predominantly male, labour on its own land, possibly supplemented at peak periods of the farming cycle by non-monetarised reciprocal exchanges of labour. In such households economic activities such as *chicha* production might either complement or supplement agricultural production, while in women-headed households, on the other hand, they are likely to play a more central role in securing the needs for social reproduction. Critically, however, it is clear that while there are few opportunities for men to sell their labour power locally, there are even fewer for women. A glance at the regional labour market confirms the importance - for those women, for example, who seek to secure a cash income to meet household needs - that they must generate their own repertoire of activities in response to local opportunities.

Within the wider regional economy, with its low level of industrial and commercial capitalist development, the possibilities for social and, therefore, spatial mobility are severely restricted. The long-established dominance of small-scale enterprises within the Cochabamba region generates little demand for wage labour and leaves little opportunity for self-created occupations within the urban economy for migrants from the highlands. Consequently, for young rural women there are few alternatives to domestic service in the homes of the urban middle class, and for young men occasional work as low-paid labourers in construction, although since the early 1980s increasing numbers have taken advantage of the 'boom' in coca-leaf production in the Chapare.[7]

These restricted opportunities for wage labour underline how inappropriate it is to universalise a rural labour process as characterised by a tendency toward proletarianisation. Rather, in many areas it is possible to identify the reproduction of the rural economy in terms of an intensification of commodity relations which may involve processes both of agricultural specialisation and economic diversification. That such apparently divergent, even contradictory, processes may be pursued simultaneously by households with different levels of resource endowments underlines the need to adopt a more flexible, empirically sensitive framework that recognises the ways by which rural households construct and develop repertoires of livelihood activities.

Unfortunately, however, there is too little institutional recognition of the importance of economic diversification amongst rural households, especially the poorest. Interventions by rural development programmes often seek to encourage the further intensification of agricultural commodity production, which in many areas may be already approaching levels that cannot possibly be sustained given the fragility of the environmental resource base and the technology used to exploit it. Such interventions may also place greater store on strengthening the sphere of production dominated by men rather than those activities controlled by women. By encouraging increased agricultural specialisation, for example, in preference to programmes that widen the opportunities for income-generation, this form of intervention serves to exacerbate the vulnerability of households to climatic and other natural hazards (such as hail, pest and disease) and fluctuations in market prices. Such risks and uncertainty further underline the vital importance that non-agricultural, income-generating activities perform for meeting the needs of household reproduction.

The preceding discussion of *chicha* production was intended to provide an illustration of the enterprise and resilience of rural households, especially those with the fewest resources. It highlights the extraordinary diversity of household forms and the variety of roles that a single activity, such as the brewing of *chicha*, can perform for different household units. Yet the kinds of interventions promoted by the state and other development agencies often fail to give sufficient attention to the essential feature of such diversity. As the majority of agricultural and other kinds of small-scale commodity production throughout the south is in the hands of poor household enterprises, it would seem both appropriate and necessary to give greater attention and material resources to the ways by which such forms of production can be supported and the livelihoods of rural households strengthened and sustained.

Notes

1. The hacienda, or large agricultural estate worked by peasant labour under a service-tenure arrangement, dominated the Bolivian countryside up to the National Revolution of 1952. The following year a Law of Agrarian Reform was introduced to break with the old order. However, in general terms the Reform consolidated the pattern of *de facto* landholding that existed before the Revolution, by providing titles to peasant households

occupying usufruct plots, though outlawed all labour service obligations (see Pearse 1975).

2. A *chicheria* is usually just a ground floor room of the producer's house where *chicha* is sold and consumed. The availability of *chicha* in the Cochabamba Valleys is marked by a small flag fluttering from a pole outside the house.
3. See McCall (1987) for details of *pombe* in Tanzania and Saul (1981) for an analysis of sorghum beer (*raam*) manufacture in rural Burkina Faso.
4. There are two posts of *alcalde* in Santa Rosa, usually occupied every year by older men. It is an exclusively ceremonial post whose functions appear to be limited to distributing *coca* leaf and *chicha* at times of *fiestas*.
5. When there is no *chicha* many rural Bolivians drink a potent cane spirit. The consumption of alcohol and the incidence of alcohol-related illness in the rural Andes is a subject that deserves serious research attention.
6. In 1980 this author attended the annual auction of the rights to collect the *chicha* tax (*licitacion del impuesto de la chicha*). Given that the overwhelming majority of *chicha* producers are women, it was interesting to observe that the auction was almost exclusively attended by men, many of whom appeared unsettled by my presence. It was later learned that they feared I would participate in the auction and not only raise the bidding to a level more accurately reflecting the true value of the tax collection rights, but also even outbid one or two of them. This would have denied to some what has effectively become 'historic rights of tribute' amongst this collection of landowners, merchants and other members of the rural elite.
7. Many young rural migrants have been attracted to work in the cocaine kitchens as *pisadores*, working barefoot in pits filled with coca leaves, kerosene and sulphuric acid in the preliminary processing stage to produce cocaine paste (Sage, 1989).

References

Beneria, L. and Sen, G. (1988) Accumulation, Reproduction and Women's Role in Economic Development: Boserup Revisited, in Pahl R. E. (ed.) *On Work: Historical, Comparative and Theoretical Approaches*. Oxford, Basil Blackwell, 355–71.

Booth, D. (1985) Marxism and Development Sociology: Interpreting the Impasse, *World Development*, vol. 13, no. 7: 761–87.

Bourque, S. and Warren, K. (1981) *Women of the Andes: Patriarchy and Social Change in Two Peruvian Towns*. Ann Arbor: The University of Michigan Press.

Buttel, F. and Goodman D. (1989) Class, State, Technology and International Food Regimes: An Introduction to Recent Trends in the Sociology and Political Economy of Agriculture, *Sociologia Ruralis*, vol. XXIX, no 2: 86–92.

Chambers, R. (1983) *Rural Development. Putting the last first*. Harlow, Essex, Longman.

Deere, C. D. (1978) The Differentiation of the Peasantry and Family Structure: A Peruvian Case Study. *Journal of Family History*, vol. 3, no. 4: 422–38.

Figueroa, A. (1982) Production and Market Exchange in Peasant Economies: The Case of the Southern Highlands of Peru, in Lehmann, D. (ed.) *Ecology and Exchange in the Andes*. Cambridge: Cambridge University Press.

Friedmann, H. (1980) Household Production and the National Economy: Concepts for the Analysis of Agrarian Formations, *Journal of Peasant Studies*, vol. 7, no. 2: 158–84.

Friedmann, H. (1986) Patriarchal Commodity Production, in MacEwan Scott, A. (ed.) *Rethinking Petty Commodity Production*, Social Analysis Special Issue Series, no. 20: 47–55.

Goodman, D. and Redclift M. (1981) *From Peasant to Proletarian: Capitalist Development and Agrarian Transitions*. Oxford, Basil Blackwell.

Guyer, J. and Peters, P. (1987) Introduction, in Guyer J. and Peters P. (eds) Conceptualising the Household: Issues of Theory and Policy in Africa, *Development and Change*, vol. 18, no. 2: 197–213.

Harris, O. (1981) Households as Natural Units, in Young, K., Wolkowitz, C. and McCullagh, R. (eds) *Of Marriage and the Market: Women's Subordination in International Perspective*, London, CSE Books, 49–68.

IESE (1975) Impuesto a la chicha. Unpublished mimeo. Instituto de Estudios Socio-economicos. Universidad Mayor de San Simòn, Cochabamba, Bolivia.

Janvry, A. de (1981) *The Agrarian Question and Reformism in Latin America*. London, The Johns Hopkins University Press.

Lehmann, D. (1982) After Chayanov and Lenin: New Paths of Agrarian Capitalism, *Journal of Development Economics*, vol. 11: 133–61.

Long, N. (1977) Commerce and Kinship in the Peruvian Highlands, in Bolton, R. and Meyer, E. (eds) *Andean Kinship and Marriage*, Washington, D.C., American Anthropological Association Special Publication, No. 7.

Long, N. (1984) Introduction in Long, N. (ed.) *Family and Work in Rural Societies: Perspectives on Non-Wage Labour*. London, Tavistock, 1–29.

Long, N. (1986) Commoditization: Thesis and Antithesis, in Long, N., van der Ploeg, J.D., Curtin, C., and Box, L. *The Commoditization Debate: Labour Process, Strategy and Social Network*, Wageningen, The Agricultural University, 8–23.

Long, N. (1988) Sociological Perspectives on Agrarian Development and State Intervention, in Hall, A. and Midgley, J. (eds) *Development Policies: Sociological Perspectives*. London, Routledge.

Long, N. (ed) (1989) *Encounters at the Interface: A Perspective on Social Discontinuities in Rural Development*. Wageningen, The Agricultural University.

Long, N. and Roberts, B. (eds) (1978) *Peasant Co-operation and Capitalist Expansion in Central Peru*. Austin, Texas, University of Texas.

Long, N. and Roberts, B. (1984) *Miners, Peasants and Entrepreneurs: Regional Development in the Central Highlands of Peru*. Cambridge, Cambridge University Press.

Long, N., van der Ploeg, J. D., Curtin, C. and Box, L., (1986) *The Commoditization Debate: Labour Process, Strategy and Social Network*. Wageningen, The Agricultural University.

Mackintosh, M. (1988) Domestic Labour and the Household, in Pahl, R. E. (ed) *On Work: Historical, Comparative and Theoretical Approaches*, Oxford, Basil Blackwell, 392–406.

Mallon, F. E. (1983) *The Defense of Community in Peru's Central Highlands: Peasant Struggle and Capitalist Transition, 1860–1940*. New Jersey, Princeton University Press.

McCall, M. (1987) Carrying Heavier Burdens but Carrying Less Weight: Some Implications of Villagization for Women in Tanzania, in Henshall Momsen, J. and Townsend J. (eds) *Geography of Gender in the Third World*, London, Hutchinson, 192–214.

Oppong, C. (1982) Family Structure and Women's Reproductive and Productive Roles: Some Conceptual and Methodological Issues, in Anker, R., Buvinic, M. and Youssef, N. (eds) *Women's Roles and Population Trends in the Third World*, London, Croom Helm, 133–50.

Pearse, A. (1975) *The Latin American Peasant*. London, Frank Cass.

Sage, C. (1989) Drugs and Economic Development in Latin America: A study in the Political Economy of Cocaine in Bolivia, in Ward, P. (ed.), *Corruption, Development and Inequality: Soft Touch or Hard Graft?* London, Routledge, 38–57.

Sage, C. (1990) *Petty Producers, Potatoes and Land: A Case Study of Agrarian Change in the Cochabamba Serrania, Bolivia*. Ph.D Thesis, University of Durham.

Sànchez, R. (1982) The Andean Economic System and Capitalism, in Lehmann, D. (ed) *Ecology and Exchange in the Andes*. Cambridge, Cambridge University Press, 157–90.

Saul, M. (1981) Beer, Sorghum and Women: Production for the Market in Rural Upper Volta, *Africa*, vol. 51:746–64.

Scott, A. M. (ed.) (1986) *Rethinking Petty Commodity Production, Social Analysis*, Special Issue Series, no. 20: 1-10.

Smith, C. (1986) Reconstructing the Elements of Petty Commodity Production, in Scott, A. M. (ed.) *Rethinking Petty Commodity Production, Social Analysis*, Special Issue Series, no. 20: 29–46.

Smith, G. (1985) Reflections on the Social Relations of Simple Commodity Production, *Journal of Peasant Studies* vol. 13, no. 1:99–108.

Vandergeest, P. and Buttel, F. (1988) Marx, Weber, and Development Sociology: Beyond the Impasse, *World Development*, vol. 16, no. 6: 683–95.

CHAPTER 5

Rediscovering Small-Scale Enterprise in Rural Hungary

Imre Kovach

In the dramatically changing Hungarian economy and society of the 1980s small enterprises represent one of the elements that appear deeply different from the essential redistribution-based features of the Stalinist and post-Stalinist economic and social structure. The revival of private and family enterprises in the non-state and non-cooperative sectors that began twenty or twenty-five years ago and their partial strengthening have significantly contributed to the emergence of the particular features, such as high living standards, abundant consumer goods and personal autonomy, which distinguish Hungary from other Eastern European countries.

The revival of autonomous and family enterprises has proved to be especially strong and effective in rural society. The rural population, being disfavoured in almost all orthodox economic and social spheres, has been able to ease a part of those disadvantages by means of autonomous enterprises. This chapter attempts to describe the revival of those enterprise modes and forms that have made Hungary different from other countries in Eastern Europe, and have led to important changes in society, power and politics.

As the concept of 'rural' as well as that of 'enterprise' have special meaning in Hungary (and in Eastern Europe), discussion of the revival of rural small enterprises must begin with an interpretation of these two notions. In the next part of the chapter, the concrete forms of countryside enterprises will be discussed. The conclusions will give a review of social-political changes related to the revival of such enterprises.

Rural regions and small enterprises

The meaning of 'rural' in Hungary

The differentiation of the concepts 'rural' and 'urban' in Hungary is of great importance in respect of administration. Contemporary politics and culture actually divide Hungarian society into two parts. The proportion of those living in rural areas (homesteads, villages, provincial towns) amounts to about 40 per cent of the total population (Figure 5.1). The 'urban' and the 'rural' coincide with considerable differences in such crucial things as the share in development funds, infrastructure, education and school networks, cultural facilities, material conditions of life, employment, and so forth.

In respect of the administration, the distinction made between 'urban' and 'rural' is important because Hungarian economic policy is very redistributive in nature. Profit is withheld, to a considerable extent, from the individual units of production, enterprises, co-operatives and regions, in order to redistribute it, as well as other resources, according to specific policy considerations. One of the considerations is the administrative status of settlements. The ranking of settlements into categories is subject to their administrative functions, population and state of infrastructural supply. In many cases, this administrative ranking is more or less arbitrary. Villages as administrative units are merged or detached by administrative measures, administrative decisions make cities from big villages and vice versa. The administrative category, to which a place is allocated, can essentially determine the extent to which the individual settlement is given development funds redistributed by the central authorities. The rural–provincial town regions are always at a disadvantage as compared to big cities and industrial centres. The disfavoured position of the rural population is one of the most significant social discriminations in Hungary. An essentially slower and less powerful urbanisation than that in the West has resulted in an ambiguous modernisation of the countryside, and many specific rural features still survive, even in the 'urban' areas.

From the middle of the twentieth century onwards, industrialisation and

Figure 5.1 The proportion of rural population in Hungary (%)

1870	1949	1960	1970	1980	1989
70.1	62.0	60.3	53.6	46.8	40.5

Note: The data follow the current administrative scheme; accordingly, those of 1870 refer to the post-World War II territory of Hungary, instead of the then Hungarian Monarchy. The change of settlements' administrative status does not necessarily indicate their urbanisation. Town status has been achieved frequently under political pressure, and not as a result of an actual urbanisation.

(*Source*: Central Statistical Office, Budapest, 1989)

urbanisation have been encouraged by particular political programmes. After World War II, the political system and the social structure of the country changed. The point of the change was that a stronger-than-ever central state came into being with the intention of managing the economic and settlement policy of the country by central planning methods. This economic and settlement policy aimed primarily at a rapid development of large-scale industry (especially heavy industry) and an accelerated urbanisation. In line with these goals the social structure was also meant to be transformed, in order to have a higher ratio of industrial workers. In 1968, a less centralised and more market-oriented economic political reform was introduced, giving rural areas a greater share. The central development of industries and cities remained poorly related. Industrialisation did not bring about an equivalent increase in urbanisation. While the rate of those employed in the agrarian sphere declined to about half of its previous level (to 22 per cent), the proportion of those living in rural regions remained as high as 45 per cent. In short, the urban population has grown, the occupational structure has transformed, but many elements of the old urban-rural relationship still survive.

The equalisation of the occupational structure between urban and rural populations represents a new trait in the urban-rural relationship, as the rate of industrial workers has increased within the rural population. In Hungary, some fifty per cent of industrial workers live in rural areas, although white-collar workers are more heavily concentrated in the cities. There are nearly one million commuters. Commuting from the rural to the urban areas came about as a side-effect of industrialisation. Urban industry gains its supply of labour from the rural areas but these people, who work in city industries, live in the countryside and often maintain very intensive part-time farming.

Two remarkable changes have marked the rural regions in the emerging rural-urban relationship. Industrialisation and the establishing of co-operatives in the late 1950s has resulted in the transformation of the social structure of rural areas, particularly of the traditional peasantry. Following the break-up of the big landed estates after World War II, during the period 1959 to 1963 the authorities encouraged and forced people to join the agricultural co-operatives. Over 95 per cent of small-holders and middle peasants entered the co-ops. It was at this time that migration to the cities and the transformation of the occupational structure accelerated as masses of the young generation gave up working in agriculture and went into various industrial occupations.

The second major change took place from the late 1960s onwards and involved relatively rapid technical modernisation of rural areas. Many new houses were built, people bought increasing numbers of modern household machines, consumer electronics and other products. The order and the habits of traditional peasant life disintegrated, even disappeared. With the spread of radio and TV sets, the emergence of occupationally heterogenous families and the spread of commuting, the pattern of rural–urban values and ways of life began to change.

Despite the transformation of the occupational structure and the growth of urbanisation, many traditional socio-economic elements have endured in the rural areas. The most important of these is perhaps the current 'under-development', as compared to the urban parts of the country. In the countryside, for example, fossil fuels and electricity are more expensive, infrastructure is much less developed, the same job is paid less, and there is poorer access to education and training.

A surviving feature of rural areas is people's involvement in agricultural production. Although the rate of those employed in agriculture has very much diminished a variety of people, including white-collar workers, participate in small-scale agrarian production in the countryside. By the early 1980s, participation in the so-called second economy, on top of a full-time job, had become widespread. Eighty per cent of heads of household are involved in the second economy, offering extra income for the household (see Szelenyi, 1988; Kovach, 1988). Today, earnings from a main occupation are hardly enough to live on, and they are by no means enough to save from, to build a house or to buy a flat. Activity in the second economy is the only way to achieve better living standards, but it is strictly limited to small-scale farming in the Hungarian countryside. It is an absolutely legalised, tax-free gross income (HUF 400,000 a year) representing about four times as much as the average income earned in a main occupation.

The idea of small enterprise

Like most countries in Eastern Europe, Hungary has lived through radical economic and structural changes since World War II (see Szelenyi, 1988). Having supressed a popular uprising the government reorganised the small farms' sector, the last private sector of the economy, into co-operatives (*kolkhozes*) between 1959 and 1963. Between 1949 and 1963, the number of artisans and retailers working in the legal private sector fell from 8.1 to 1.7 per cent of active earners, while the number of independent farmers decreased from 56.7 to 1.3 per cent during the same period.

The centralisation of control over the economy and social reproduction ceased at the beginning of the 1960s as a temporary economic expedient, but, by then, the role of autonomous economic activities and market mechanisms had been severely run down. However, neither the autonomous economic activities of households, nor certain market-oriented activities could be effectively stopped. Both industry and agriculture brought under state control proved unable to meet public needs in food, industrial products or services. People fought against shortage by means of producing goods and services for their own use and for exchange on the market. However, following the changes in political conditions at home and abroad, and the Reform of 1968, the number of small plants and small-scale ventures, especially in the field of consumer goods production, also increased. The process began in agriculture, then expanded into the commercial and industrial sectors from the second half of the 1970s.

The constant housing shortage provided another stimulus to such activity, inciting more and more people to build their own flat without state assistance with building costs. The rising rate of inflation from 1979 (over 10 per cent a year) led to a decrease in the real value of wages. This coincided with growing expectations of higher standards of living associated with the 'Western way of life'. In conjunction, these trends encouraged an ever increasing number of households to look for ways of gaining extra income. The pursuit of income outside the hours of paid employment and of goods to directly supplement household consumption had become widespread by the early 1980s. According to statistics for 1982, some 75 to 80 per cent of the

Figure 5.2 Distribution of households in rural and urban areas grouped by source of extra income, in 1982 (%)

Groups*	Rural	Urban	Total
1	16.5	83.5	24.9
2	68.0	72.0	27.4
3	84.7	15.3	17.3
4	1.6	98.4	0.7
5	11.1	88.9	3.9
6	9.0	91.0	1.3
7	10.7	89.3	5.3
8	8.4	91.6	1.8
9	54.5	45.5	3.7
10	58.2	41.8	5.0
11	49.9	50.1	0.9
12	74.6	25.4	2.8
13	83.4	16.6	4.2
14	79.8	20.2	0.9
Total	50.4	49.6	100.0

***Key**

1 no additional incomes, only a full-time job in the public sector
2 extra income from self-supporting agrarian production, added to the total income of household
3 extra income yielded by marketing the products of small-scale farming activities
4 additional part-time job in the public sector
5 overtime work in full-time job
6 additional semi-legal income (e.g. tips)
7 extra income yielded by some activity in a non-agrarian field of the second economy
8 joint occurrence of 4, 5, 6, 7
9 joint occurrence of 2, 4, 5, 6
10 joint occurrence of 2, 7
11 joint occurrence of 2, 4, 5, 6, 7
12 joint occurrence of 3, 4, 5, 6
13 joint occurrence of 3, 7
14 joint occurrence of 3, 4, 5, 6, 7

(*Source*: Boros, 1984)

population over the age of 18 were doing productive and paid activities besides their full-time job (see Figure 5.2).

Hungarian economists quickly responded to these developments in the research literature by inventing the term 'second economy'. A long debate followed on the interpretation of the second economy, and consensus has never been reached. Here, I adapt the definition of Gabor and Galasi (1982), who state:

> By the second economy, taken in the wide sense, we mean the ways of using one's capacity to work outside the state sector of the economy, and all the redistribution processes that are taking place outside the socially organised distribution of incomes.

Accordingly, the following items are included in the second sphere of economy and distribution:

> (a) activities in the legalised private sector;
> (b) productive and service activities of 'hidden' employees and outworkers; illegal trade paying no tax; those who do not carry out their professional service activity in co-operatives or on a family-business basis, but who, as entrepreneurs or contractors, offer their services on the market;
> (c) commodity producing and subsistence farming on small or large pieces of land and landed property, making individually operated household farms on a family basis or with hired labour;
> (d) those incomes of the population, connected with activities exercised within the organisations of the state sector, at work places, etc, which take the form of a 'tip', 'bribe' or 'sop';
> (e) a number of further forms of gaining incomes, groupings outside the state-organised framework, e.g. renting private buildings or parts of state-owned housing estate and property by people, loan transactions between private persons; all kinds of contracts and agreements having payment/income implications (pp 17–18).

Owing to the nature of the second economy, reliable data are not available for all forms or for a long time period, but those shown in Figure 5.3 for the years 1984–1987 can be taken as a reasonable estimate.

If we simply combine the data in Figure 5.3, we cannot get the precise number of those involved in the second economy. We have no data on those who receive 'invisible' incomes; it is also possible that some households are involved in several simultaneous activities in the second economy. More than half of small farmers participate in one or other form of activity in the second economy. Fifty-five per cent of tradespeople working in the legal private sector live in their own houses where they also undertake small-scale farming. As an estimate, about 90 per cent of Hungarian households are 'pluri-active', in terms of their generation of income.

The extension of the second economy is characterised by the fact that,

Figure 5.3 Participants in different forms of activities in the second economy, 1984–1987

Small-scale industry and retail trade	150,000 persons
Trade and public catering units operated on lease-contracts	36,000 persons
Private room letting, house letting	110,000 persons
New small-scale ventures (working pools within big companies, economic working units, civil partnerships)	300,000 persons
Co-operative specialised groups (with industrial, agricultural or service activities)	80,000 persons
Unpermitted, illegal services	270,000 persons
Private housing	900,000 persons
Agricultural small-scale production	3,000,000 persons

(*Source*: Kovach, 1988)

according to an estimate for 1985, 45 per cent of the total income of the population originated from the first economy, 35 per cent from the second economy and 20 per cent from pensions or allowances. A consequence of the economic crisis and accelerating inflation since 1985 is that an ever growing number of citizens is dependent upon services at home and the production of food for their own consumption. Thus, these shares have probably changed since 1985 increasing the significance of the second economy. The estimates in Figure 5.4 show the increases in invisible incomes in the 1980s.

The importance of the second economy is also represented by the fact that the increase in national income during the 1980s is attributed solely to activities in this sphere of the economy. Little more than half of total agricultural production, for example, is produced by small-scale farms. It is necessary to emphasise that, besides the extension of activities in the second economy, an overwhelming majority of participants are employed in the first economy too. The Hungarian people work the longest hours in Europe – including both the first and second economy, 10–12 hours a day. Moreover, as Figures 5.3 and 5.4 show, an important element of the second economy (illegal and non-market forms) cannot be considered enterprise.

In this chapter I use the terms 'enterprise'/'entrepreneur' as established in Hungarian conditions and research literature, which is, of course, different from that of market economies. There have been long debates in the Hungarian literature, without any consensus, about who can be regarded as

Figure 5.4 The volume of 'invisible' incomes in Hungary (in billion forints)

'Gratitude money' (doctors)	7–8
Bribes	29–22
Renting out flats, holiday cottages	6–7
Hidden transactions in real estate	17–20
Money-lending, usury	3
Illegal currency dealings	2–3
Stealing, misappropriation	14–16
Moonlighting	28–29
Tax evasion	12–14

Note: US$ 100 = approximately HUF 6,500
(*Source*: Galasi and Sik, 1988)

an entrepreneur and what sorts of economic activities can be considered enterprise. In the view of the Hungarian public, all kinds of economic activities are generally regarded as enterprise which yield legal income and/or material goods outside the redistributive (state and co-operative) sectors. Accordingly, I use the term in this sense, always indicating the concrete forms of enterprise.

In 1987, about 36,000 new enterprises, 160–165,000 artisans and 36,000 shopkeepers had business permits. According to estimates based on 1982 data, about 17 per cent, that is 374,000 units, out of 2,200,000 households involved in agricultural production, operated as enterprises. On 31 July 1989 as many as 59,708 artisans worked in the countryside (KIOSZ, 1988). Such precise data are not available on shopkeepers, but from the earlier statistics considered, we can calculate about 8–10,000 small traders in the countryside. There are no proper data on the new types of small businesses operating in the countryside either, but reasonable estimates suggest 20–25 per cent of the overall number must be working in villages or small towns – that means about 7,000 organisations. Eighty-three per cent of genuine agricultural small enterprises are functioning, in the countryside – that means 347,820 units. Altogether there are 420–425 thousand or so small enterprises in the countryside that we can take into account; at least 75 per cent of their members or employees are doing these activities as part-timers, while having a full job in the state or co-operative sector.

Forms of rural enterprise

Small-scale production in agriculture

In Hungary (and in other Eastern European countries) agriculture still presents the greatest opportunities for autonomous forms of production and private enterprise. The contemporary pattern of large and small-scale agricultural production is the outcome of the socialisation of the agrarian sector, begun in 1947–1948, and reaching its peak between 1959 and 1963, when 97 per cent of peasants, who had until then been working on their own, were organised into *kolkhoz*-type co-operatives. Despite the organisation of the co-operatives the role of small-scale farming and household-based food production had still not been eliminated by the early 1960s. The gradual closure of local markets, the initial shortages of large-scale agriculture, the absorption of labourpower, the slowing down of migration towards industrial cities, and so forth, all encouraged the self-provisioning of food by those working in agriculture, as well as production for local markets. Realising this situation, the national authorities provided opportunities in the statutes of co-operatives for 'household farming' which, it was thought, would be limited to self-provisioning, but in fact exceeded that role from the start. In the 1960s, production for sale was still uncommon but small-scale producers remained sensitive to market changes and the market-orientedness

Figure 5.5 Small farms' share of agricultural production by various products, in 1984

		percentage share
Cereals		9.1
out of them:	maize	18.9
	legumes	11.7
	tobacco	77.9
	poppy	75.0
	potato	73.3
Vegetables		62.0
out of them:	cabbage	70.9
	carrot	67.2
	onion	65.5
	cucumber	95.3
	tomato	69.6
	green pepper	84.4
Fruits		59.4
out of them:	apple	49.5
	pear	65.2
	cherry	91.1
	sour-cherry	72.2
	plum	90.2
Grape		56.4
Beef-cattle		15.4
Pig for slaughter		57.2
Poultry		44.3
Hare		97.7
Cow's milk		25.6
Hen's egg		60.7
Honey		99.9

(*Source*: Kovach, 1988)

of small producers strengthened and became better articulated as a result of the radical reorganisation of agriculture in 1968. From the early 1970s, the strengthening of exports from agriculture and a more lively domestic market provided a powerful incentive to produce for the market. As a consequence, within one decade, the proportion of small-scale farms producing for sale rose threefold. In the 1970s, the gross production of small farms reached half of that of the large-scale farms (see Figure 5.5).

While in 1970 the percentage of products sold on the market was 37 per cent of the overall production of small farmers, in 1980 this proportion had risen to 60 per cent, a historical record in the twentieth century history of small-scale agriculture in Hungary. The elimination of some traditional bases of small-scale production, namely the ownership of land and the means of production, resulted in rapid changes in the numbers involved in small-scale production and in the volume and range of products. This situation was further complicated by the fact that a producer was no longer tied to one agricultural market but might be participating in several markets at the same time. These conditions allowed many people to engage in small-scale agricultural production from social groups which had had no previous involvement in this sector. As a consequence of the ever growing demand for extra income and direct consumption, masses of people working in other fields of the economy began agricultural production on a part-time basis.

Production-for-sale by small-scale agricultural units is severely impeded by the legal regulation of the private ownership of, and private market in, land. It is also impeded by the unfavourable market prices for small farmers and the general shortage of capital and infrastructure. Ninety to 95 per cent of small agricultural producers are employed, part- or full-time, in other sectors of the first economy. In this situation, where production for the market and for family consumption are not the only ways of gaining income and saving money, decisions made on the volume and methods of production depend on the effectiveness of participation in other sectors and fields of economic activity. Besides, or rather in consequence of, the limitation of the market and the pluri-activity of most agricultural households engaged in small production, the behaviour of small producers combining traditional producing practices with flexibility, also acts as a regulating factor in production for the market.

Today's limited and regulated market is not able to comprehensively integrate small-scale production. Forty per cent of the products from these smallholdings do not get to the market, they are simply consumed by the producers themselves. Most small farmers are dependent on the services of the large-scale farms which provide much of the transportation, seeds, animal food, new stocks, chemicals and so on. Less than two per cent of small farms have no economic relations with large units. From the middle of the 1970s onwards, many large-scale farms have seen an involvement in the production and marketing activities of small farms as a good commercial opportunity. They have tried to gain a monopoly in the marketing, processing and control of goods produced in the small-scale holdings. This process of incorporation has proceeded quite easily because the large organisations often monopolise access to the market. This process of incorporation means that, with many products, the greater the increase in the production of a small farm, the higher the degree of integration entailed. Many of the biggest small producers organise their production around the deals offered by the large-scale state or co-operative farms.

There have been three basic forms of part-time farms in 1980s: (a) those producing for self-provisioning (44%), (b) traditional, peasant-type (38%) and (c) farmer-type, entrepreneurial (18%).

(a) Self-provisioning type part-time farms

Here, production takes place in the garden around the house, and in the back-yard; the aim is to produce as much food as possible for household-consumption. Any surplus may be sold, but production for exchange does not determine the style of farming. The main products tend to be vegetables, poultry and pigs, and, less frequently, fruit. In some households one or two cows may also be kept. Production methods, especially for livestock, involve predominantly traditional technologies. The costs, enterprises and labour of the household and the small farm are not separated, the farming operation being actively determined by the needs and opportunities of the household. The production of food is of primary importance and consequently, although small farms may exchange labour and contacts with other units of this kind, there is no relationship between agricultural market conditions and the functioning of these small farms. This pattern of activity is a common practice even for those without qualifications, those who are not forced to do it by their financial position, and those who have no background in agriculture.

A variation of this type of part-time farming has been developing since the late 1960s. Some tens of thousands of hobby-gardens have been marked out in regions where one would rarely have encountered holiday-makers before. Around country towns a ring of hobby-gardens has grown up. For example, around Pecs, in the centre of Southern Transdanubia, there are approximately 6,000 such hobby-gardens (Baksai, 1983). The development of this kind of part-time farming is a consequence of considerable changes in life-style. Houses without gardens in small country towns have been extended over the years by building additional storeys, while immigration from the villages and provinces to large cities has increased. In addition, from the late 1970s onwards, spending leisure-time in 'natural' settings has become a general feature of modern living, a trend which has included the cultivation of hobby- and holiday-gardens. The growth of these spare-time activities has been supported by rising standards of living, the accumulation of capital which can be invested in them and the spread of private car ownership which has brought such gardens within reach.

Although self-provisioning of food is an important objective, the quantity of marketed products may well exceed that of traditional self-consumption. In the case of this form of part-time farming, household and business affairs are separated in every respect. The place of production does not coincide with that of residence; work is done in spare time, apart from other household activities. This is indicated by the fact that, while in the self-provisioning small farms it has traditionally been women who work in the garden and keep the animals, in the case of hobby-gardens it is typically the male family members who take this role. Separation between household and enterprise is manifested in the administration of funds too. Spare-time production is based on a rational calculation of costs and products even if the primary aim is not marketing but consuming the products. Separation of household and enterprise is made easier by the fact that production here is not an everyday activity, but usually limited to weekends. This precludes the keeping of animals in this form of part-time farming. The major products are vegetables, fruit, grapes and wine.

(b) Peasant type part-time farms

The fundamental role of this category of part-time farms is commodity production but, like traditional peasant farms, they also consume some of their own produce. The site of production could be either the ground around the house, enclosed lands, a household plot or a parcel of land taken on lease. They have several products, depending on the constraints of the market and self-provisioning. Production itself is far from being specialised, nevertheless, one or two products tend to be produced in large quantities. The activities and finances of household and enterprise are occasionally separated, but they basically constitute one economic unit. Finances are based on a rational calculation of costs and products, although labour costs are mostly disregarded. Some of them, however, are subject to local customs and farming practices which are preserved through the use of traditional technologies of production.

It is the duality of commodity production and self-provisioning of food that enables small farms to hold their ground against the unfavourable consequences of economic and political changes. It is this duality which preconditions the autonomy of this form of farming and lies behind the reason why these small farms do not integrate their production into that of big estates, and do not enter into sales contracts for each product. The mixed composition of production is still maintained even if a part of it proves to be less profitable. Owing to their mixed product pattern and wide business relations they can respond to changes on the market. They always can produce the most saleable goods and find the most profitable means of marketing them. Most phases of production are undertaken on the small farm in order to sustain this market activity.

This form of production, particularly, retains the structural traditions of small peasant farms that had been organised both for self-provisioning and commodity production. This is the most popular form of production even today, representing the highest single share of all forms of small-scale production at 38.6 per cent. In addition to the transmission of farming patterns, its survival is all the more likely given that the large majority of the small-scale producing population have no other means to get extra income except in part-time farming.

(c) Entrepreneurial type part-time farms

About 17 or 18 per cent of all small producers are working as farmer-entrepreneurs. This is particularly characteristic of specialised stock-breeding. Production takes place in the buildings and with the labour of the family and household engaged in production, but their work is only a part of the process, fattening in most cases. Products are sold through some large company which, in turn, provides the farmers with young animals and animal food at contracted prices. In these conditions production for self-provisioning is more uncertain. Owing to the specialised nature of production, the division between the household and the enterprise is sharp, despite their close proximity. The entrepreneur's production is largely integrated into the production of a large company (co-operative or state farm) so that, despite the specialised production and the rational calculation, they do not resemble the typical Western enterprise either.

In a second variation of this type of farm, the small producer/large company relationship is also important. The company provides the animals, machines, credit, seedlings and so on needed to start production, and it also keeps in hand processing and marketing of the products. Unlike the first type, this is a true enterprise because the most important steps in production are controlled by the small producer, whose investment and financial transactions are independent from the large company. The small producer here contributes not only labour, expertise and buildings to the enterprise, but frequently risks his or her capital. The entrepreneur works as full-time farmer and often employs additional labour, beyond the family members working in business. The purest form of this kind of enterprise is the chicken-farm in which 10 to 50 thousand broilers are bred a year, in fully mechanised poultry-houses. The actual value of such a farm amounts to 15–16 years' income of an average family living on a salary. Goose-breeding is the most popular, besides chicken-farms, while in plant cultivation grapes and fruit are the dominant products.

The enterprise organised for producing only for marketing is a form of agricultural small production that began to gain ground in the early 1980s. In its basic characteristics it meets the requirements of a classic small enterprise, with the sole difference perhaps being that the enterprising/producing household undertakes a lot of physical work too. A small enterprise requires not only a high level of agricultural expertise, but also knowledge of financial and commercial management. It is the small producers who carry out all parts of the production process, making farming a full-time job. In these market enterprises, people produce vegetables and fruit because the fodder requirements of large-scale production cannot be covered by a household unit, due to the limitations on land-use imposed by the state. Typical of this form of small enterprise are greenhouses or foil production systems.

These examples demonstrate the main kinds of agricultural small scale enterprise and the production output of three main forms of farm organisation. In the first, highly integrated type of enterprise the unit will produce 80 to 150 pigs, or 15 to 20 oxen a year. The second category characterises many chicken-farms, but also horticultural units of one to three acres. The third tends to involve foil or greenhouse cultivation of some 700 to 1,500 square metres. The net income from such enterprises always amounts to several times the average Hungarian annual household income in all three cases.

In addition to agricultural cases, rural areas are characterised by a strong tradition of small craft enterprises. According to the yearly report of the National Union of Artisans and the data of the Central Statistical Office, the number of those with a permit to work as independent craftspeople increases every year. While in 1987 the number of those working as full-time or part-time independent craftspeople was 152,325, in 1988 their number rose to 158,930 and by the end of July 1989 to 167,827. However, this increase comes from the growing number of craftspeople working in cities, rising from 91,834 in 1987 to 97,144 in 1988, and by the end of July 1989 to 108,114. Over the same period, the number of craftspeople living in the countryside decreased by two thousand between the end of 1988 and June 1989. This decline in the countryside can be attributed to the introduction of Personal Income Tax in 1988 and the general reform of the tax situation of those living in villages, which has deteriorated more dramatically than the situation of those living in towns.

The Hungarian population is more or less equally divided between city-dwellers and village-dwellers, but that distinction is not reflected in the distribution of small enterprises. There are far fewer small craft enterprises in the countryside, despite the fact that the shortage in services is much more significant in Hungarian villages than in towns. With inflation at nearly 20 per cent a year, and an even greater decrease in real values, households have turned to self-provisioning in an ever larger range of services. In towns as well, the proportion of services met within the households is rising. But because of relatively lower wage levels in the countryside and the tradition of communal labour exchange, it is in rural Hungary that the market for small craft enterprises is shrinking the most significantly. This decline has its roots in the early transformation of the structure of artisan production in Hungary examined in the last part of the chapter. The most dynamic branches of small craft enterprise, for example, the chemical industry, paper and textiles, handicraft industries, road transport and personal services, tend to be located in towns, or to be orientated towards meeting urban markets, as a result of Hungary's particular settlement and social structures, discussed at the beginning of the chapter. The data in Figure 5.6 show the rural trade-groups with more than 1,000 members, and clearly indicate that the traditional trade-groups, by and large, show little signs of economic dynamism.

There are nearly 3,000 rural settlements in Hungary, and if we relate this to the data in Figure 5.6, an even clearer picture of the market opportunities for small rural enterprises emerges. In only one village in three can one find a plumber or a car mechanic. Nor is there a hairdresser, dressmaker, joiner, carpenter or engine fitter in every rural settlement.

Small rural craft enterprise is severely restricted by state regulation. Their

Figure 5.6 The bigger trade-groups of rural craft enterprises, 1989

	number of tradespeople
carpenter/scaffolder	1,365
builder	6,988
painter	1,828
electrician	2,879
plumber	1,086
haulier	1,724
carrier (goods)	8,584
carrier (passengers)	11,807
engine fitter	1,608
joiner	1,237
sawing worker	2,316
dressmaker	2,408
car mechanic	1,018
women's hairdresser	1,525

(*Source*: Archive of Central Statistical Office)

field of activity is limited by national government laws, on the one hand, and local council permission procedures, on the other. A long list of clauses prescribes the physical, commercial and purchasing conditions of such enterprises, supplemented by legal uncertainties and red-tape. Possibly the greatest obstacle to small craft enterprises is the taxation and social security regime. In effect, these regimes absorb between 60 and 80 percent of the gross income of small enterprises. What is left hardly covers the costs of keeping the business afloat let alone developing it. Owing to this unfavourable system of management and the shrinking market, by 1989 20 to 25 per cent of small craft enterprises had quit their business in rural areas. It is for the same reason that little more than half of small craft enterprises are run as a full-time occupation, the rest are run to supplement a main job or as a retirement occupation.

However, at the same time, a number of new kinds of enterprise have been developing. From 1982 onwards, the government has allowed some new kinds of small enterprise, including independent working pools within companies, economic working communities, civil partnerships and specialised groups. Within just a few years nearly 50,000 such organisations have been created, the intra-company independent working pool being the most popular form among them, in towns and villages alike. These pools are organised by the employees of a given company, and are dependent on the company in many respects. The pools do not own the capital they work with, but use the plant and equipment of the company after official working hours.

Their creation and economic dynamism are largely dependent on the management of the parent-company. In this sense, the working pool does not represent genuine enterprise. In effect, those joining the pool undertake to work overtime rather than to undertake independent market activity. They get orders and materials from the company, and hardly take any risk.

Since 1982, the working conditions of such intra-company working pools have been modified several times. Free use of capital no longer exists and the pools' incomes have been drained by increased taxes. Despite these difficulties, the activity of intra-company working pools gains more and more ground every year. In the countryside the main fields in which they are active are: production of agricultural machinery, metal-ware industries, house-building, various service activities and repair of domestic appliances. Specialist groups with co-operatives do industrial and servicing work for their co-operative and for other companies. They can be created within any co-operative, provided that at least five persons can guarantee their functioning, and the parent co-operative gives consent to their creation. The co-operatives' specialist groups operate effectively as intra-co-operative working pools. Nine tenths of these groups work in the building industry. This is the only new kind of enterprise form for which there is no upper limit to the personnel. The specialist group, like the intra-company working pool, has no independent legal status. The economic working community is created by private persons, on the basis of a contract of association for production, consumption or service activities. In this form of entrepreneurship, people can work as full-time workers or they can do it as a second job, as four fifths of them do. The operation of economic working communities is concentrated mainly in Budapest, with only a few operating in the countryside. Finally, civil partnerships may be created on a contract of association, but they have no legal status either. Members have a joint liability. Shops and company units are functioning in this form. For a long time, a civil partnership could not have more than 12 people, employees and trainees included. Since 1989, when this rule was modified, civil partnerships have become a popular form of enterprise for freelance intellectuals, but again they are not widespread in the countryside.

Conclusions

Rural entrepreneurs do not constitute a unified social class or group because the constant uncertainty of being an entrepreneur and the inevitable pluriactivity of entrepreneural households make this impossible. Three fifths to three quarters of entrepreneurs are part of the socialised sector and the private sector of the economy alike, they are wage-workers and lower middle-class people at once. One of the most important effects of this ambivalent existence is the lack of a distinct class identity. The emergence of a unified stratum of entrepreneurs is rendered more difficult by the fact that craftspeople and shopkeepers, as well as small agricultural producers and those participating in the new kinds of small enterprise are rapidly changing in number. Despite these changes, there are groups, for which we can demonstrate a social continuity, with two generations or more active in the same business. For example, amongst the small agricultural entrepreneurs three times as many come from a middle peasant family as amongst small agricultural producers, in general. There is also a link between the area of land owned by the parents of those operating small enterprises and the volume of production of these enterprises (Kovach, 1988). Ivan Szelenyi considers the status of small agricultural enterprises, with middle peasant origin, the most important group within a new class of entrepreneurs (Szelenyi, 1988). Among small industrialists too, a group with enterprising background can be found, but their proportion is smaller than in the agricultural case (Vajda, 1987).

There is no rural occupation in which we cannot find entrepreneurs. Though the objective of the enterprises is social in character, and the market system formed around the enterprises and the governmental economic policy encourage, even force, the entrepreneurs to spend the bigger part of their production gains on consumption, rather than re-invest it, their income usually exceeds the average level; but consumption or wealth have not become status-markers. This contradictory relationship between economic, social and wealth positions seems to guarantee a new class formation. There is no doubt that the economic position of those operating small enterprises will materialise as social capital in different ways and that the transformation of economic advantages into social privileges is really to expand and strengthen the social position of the 'entrepreneur'. Most 'entrepreneurs' are sustaining their privileged position in the social hierarchy through their production rather than consumption activities. This method of reproduction cannot be harnessed for really radical change in social inequalities because it creates capital in the economic field and this capital cannot be easily converted into social capital. Many among these enterprises are unable to culturally convert the capital obtained through production, with their incomes, in order to change their social status to their advantage. The reproduction of their position within the first and second economies can at best offer a defence against the wider order of society. In the countryside small enterprises in various sectors have a role in sustaining the social position of the socially and culturally powerless.

There is only one way of realising the real potential of rural enterprises in the Hungary of the 1990s: the extension of market relations through a series of ownership, political and social reforms. The actual steps needed for these reforms to be taken are still unknown after the first few months of the new political pluralism. To say the least, the risk is high since socio-economic and political modernisation in Hungary, where the majority of people were still peasants even half a century ago, is hardly to be expected without a transformation of the economic relations I have analysed here not to mention the contradictory and complex social consequences and impacts.

A change concerning rural enterprises which is more certain is *embourgeoisement* (see Szelenyi, 1988) – the rise into middle class status of various social groups involved in small-scale enterprise. Embourgeoisement, as I use the term, means a historical continuity of a peasant type. Among small-scale producers and entrepreneurs there is one group whose members are characterised by some particular stratification attributes historically interpretable as continuous, such as having a similar social position and origin, and larger scale agricultural production. Some agricultural small-scale producers coming from previous middle-class and rich peasant families could keep their parents' social status, making use of the profits of their intensive private farming activity. Identical processes have been observed in the case of other enterprise forms too. In my view, this status continuity, which has been associated with a change of value orientations and a total disintegration and individualisation of traditional relations, is embourgeoisement.

Besides the process of embourgeoisement concerning a limited social group, the social impact of enterprise may also be considered, as a mass phenomenon, concerning all those who have the capacity to rise above the standard of life of the poorest and most deprived social groups, by means of the incomes yielded by rural enterprises. The transmittance and slow accumulation of property may also be followed by the strengthening of embourgeoisement and social mobility. As a consequence of the lack of a powerful, traditional entrepreneurs' stratum, economic difficulties and administrative limitations on enterprises, the enterprise has only been able, during the years of a one-party system, to ease the economic and social disadvantage of rural regions. In turn, masses of full and part-time entrepreneurs have been waiting to operate genuine enterprises within the bounds of a market economy likely to come into being in the last decade of the century, owing to rapid political changes. They have the most practice and expertise possible in Eastern Europe, and most of them have no other chance of social advancement than through such private undertakings. For this reason, the future of rural regions of Hungary will be shaped by the process of embourgeoisement, whose strengths and limitations have yet to be seen.

References

Baksai, A. (1983) *Agricultural Small-scale Farming Today and Tomorrow* Budapest, Mezögazdaságí Könyvkiade (in Hungarian).

Boros, A. (1984). Family Livelihood Strategies in Both Economies, in Kovach, L. (ed) *Economy and Society* Budapest, Institute of Social Science

Galasi, P. and Gabor, R.I. (1982) *The Second Economy.* Budapest (in Hungarian).

Galasi, P. and Sik, E. (1988) Invisible Incomes in Hungary, *Social Justice,* 3–4.

Juhasz, P. (1982) *Agricultural Market, Large-Scale Farm, Small-Scale Farm.* Medvetanc (in Hungarian).

KIOSZ (1988) Report for the Central Leadership of KIOSZ (National Union of Artisans) on the number of those working as tradesmen or employed in small industry, or being members of economic working communities, in 1988 (in Hungarian).

Kovach, I. (1988) *Producers and Entrepreneurs.* Budapest, Institute of Social Science (in Hungarian).

National Labour Office (1987) *New small organizations in 1987* Budapest (in Hungarian).

Szelenyi, I. (1988) *Socialist Entrepreneurs*. New York, University of Wisconsin.
Vajda, A. (1987) Mobility of Craftsmen and Shopkeepers, *Revue of Statistics*, 1987 (in Hungarian).

CHAPTER 6

Populism and Petit Capitalism in Rural Ireland

Chris Curtin and Tony Varley

Introduction

A basic feature of development is its historic occurrence within the context of nation states. Indeed, development, in the sense of large-scale industrialisation, has more often than now been pushed ahead, in what are now the advanced capitalist states, by considerations of *national* defence or aggrandisement (Kitching, 1982: 3–4). In the post-1945 period, development based on comprehensive national-level planning and large-scale, capital intensive industrialisation became the dominant internationally accepted model in many less-developed nations (Rondinelli, 1983). Although populist-type policies, concerned with small-scale and participative development, were also sponsored by international agencies and national governments – there were in excess of 60 national community development programmes by 1960 (Holdcroft, 1982) – it was the failure of the mainstream large-scale approach to live up to expectations that was to give a real prominence to such populist-inspired alternatives as integrated rural development and basic needs programmes (Rondinelli, 1983: 57–64; Kitching, 1982: 99). No less than the mainstream large-scale model, small-scale populist-inspired development projects, however, have encountered severe difficulties at the level of implementation (Korten, 1980: 482; Rondinelli, 1983: 77–78; Murray, 1983).

Three dimensions of populism – smallness of scale, the dispersion of economic activity, and the desirability of 'participative' development – will provide the thematic focus for our discussion here. In the hands of politicians, these dimensions may be espoused either for ideological reasons that reflect egalitarian commitments (cf. Kitching, 1982: 22) or for reasons of expediency associated with popular pressure. Smallness of scale occupies pride of place in many discussions of populism. Central to Kitching's (1982: 3) conception of populism, for instance, is the pursuit of increased material well-being in the context of 'preserving a society and economy in which small-scale agricultural producers (peasants) and non-agricultural producers (artisans) remain in a large majority'. One of the three principal types of populism discussed by Canovan (1981) centres on petit capitalism and the political orientation of small proprietors who favour private property but are suspicious of big business and government.

The survival of smallholders in the advanced capitalist countries has been attributed to their capacity to improve cost-efficiency and continue to intensify production and expand output - even if the price to be paid is crippling indebtedness (Gasson *et al.*, 1988: 31–32; Tovey, 1982). At the same time, even efficient smallholders find themselves in an increasingly precarious position and their long-term survival prospects do not appear good on account of the tendency for agriculture to become dominated by larger sized production units, the increasing movement toward capital-intensiveness, and the fact that small farmers are caught in an on-going price/cost squeeze. That small producers find themselves hemmed in by measures introduced to curb overproduction adds further to their difficulties.

Much less straightforward is the question of whether smallness of scale is a liability for manufacturing industry. Weiss (1988) uses the 'Third Italy' case to argue that there are no inherent tendencies toward larger-scale in manufacturing and that states can play a critical role in encouraging and reinforcing small-scale industrial activity. Flexible specialisation theorists argue that new technology, in combination with business-related considerations, has made small-scale industrial organisation increasingly more attractive to capital (Sabel, 1982). And it can be argued - as in Murray's (1988) account of Fiat's decentralisation policy in northern Italy - that employers may adopt smaller-scale organisation as part of a labour control strategy. (See also chapter 3 in this volume.)

An important theme that reflects populist commitment to equality is the desire to escape the world of large-scale concentrated production and to build an economic and social order based on the widest possible spatial *dispersion* of economic activity. Only with a radical measure of dispersion can 'inequalities between individuals and social groups, between town and countryside, between region and region, and between nation and nation' be overcome (Kitching, 1982: 22). However pessimistic it may be about the prospects, the spatial dispersion of economic activity is a central preoccupation of modern core/periphery theory. Conventional policies that concentrate economic growth in metropolitan areas are judged to have failed to allow the benefits of growth to trickle down and spread throughout the countryside. Instead, through the operation of 'backwash effects', rural resources tend to be siphoned off by metropolitan areas, in a way that reinforces tendencies towards dual economies and increased spatial inequalities.

Core-periphery theorists are inclined to regard established forms of development in peripheral areas - especially those based on large-scale branch plant industrialisation and international tourism - with suspicion. The reasons they give are that the former tends to be vulnerable to market and technological change while the latter can result in a loss of cultural identity. As an alternative, various models of self-reliant development, based on indigenous natural and human resources and dependent on varying levels of state intervention, have been canvassed (Bryden, 1986).

Worsley (1967) has drawn attention to the emphasis many Third World states have accorded to co-operative and communitarian forms of social and economic organisation. Participation was a key ideological feature of the national community development programmes of the 1950s and later of integrated rural development. Among the claims made for participation are that grass-roots involvement accelerates social and economic progress, thus ensuring a more equitable distribution of the benefits of development; and that it is particularly appropriate for 'deprived and disadvantaged groups in small communities' (Midgley, 1986: 13–14). Yet, many obstacles to participative development can be identified. These range from local factors that may impede attempts to mobilise localities for collective action - such as the unequal distribution of property and political power, age and gender divisions etc. - to considerations related to the state. Gilbert and Ward (1984: 770) suggest, for instance, that the state's interest in promoting community action has more to do with the task of securing its own legitimacy than with any genuine commitment to improving the lot of the poor.

Certainly much evidence suggests that participative development has frequently fallen down in practice. The fact that the poor have few resources to pool may mean that those who really benefit from co-operative activity are the better-off inhabitants of Third World societies (Korten, 1980: 481; Robertson, 1984: 168). The ability of village notables to dominate the local process of development and to absorb the lion's share of the benefits was a marked feature of the Indian community development programme of the 1950s (Holdcroft, 1982). Subsequently, failure to secure adequate levels of participation has similarly marred the rural projects sponsored by international agencies and national states; Rondinelli can report that in fewer than 50 of 200 rural development projects was effective participation secured. Excluding beneficiaries from the design and formulation of projects was to result in 'severe management problems later' (Rondinelli, 1983: 77–78).

At the point of political independence in 1921–2, the new Irish state comprised a 'small, late-industrialising, peripheral economy with a long-standing labour surplus' (Kennedy, *et al.*, 1988: 130). The present-day Republic of Ireland, though it cannot be regarded as a Third World country, does not qualify as an advanced capitalist one. A recent study suggests that within the comparable family of nations - small advanced capitalist countries such as Denmark, Finland and Austria, on the one hand, and the 'semi-peripheries' such as Greece, Brazil and Argentina, on the other - Ireland's somewhat anomalous position results from its sharing 'nationalism and populist and clientist politics' with the semi-peripheral states and relatively high levels of 'per capita incomes, literacy and educational levels' with the northern European industrial states (Girvin, 1989: 9–10).

Both before and after the Anglo-Irish Treaty of 1921 granted dominion status independence to what is now the Republic of Ireland, anti-colonial nationalism was important in explaining the attraction of populist-type policies to certain strands of Irish nationalist opinion. A significant segment of pre- and post-independence Irish nationalist opinion favoured small-scale economic activity, based on farming and manufacturing industry dispersed throughout the countryside. No less than in the advanced countries (Kitching, 1982: 3), however, the elements drawn to populism have never consistently represented a majority tendency in Ireland. This is evident in the weak nationalist commitment to re-organise the economy along co-operative lines during the Anglo-Irish War (1919–21) (O'Connor, 1988: 93); the first minister for agriculture even resisted pressure to make 'a public declaration in favour of co-operation' in the 1920s (Bolger, 1977: 118).

Our three populist dimensions were nonetheless important ideologically, not least because of the manner in which they converged with some of the basic tenets of Catholic social teaching. In particular, populist policies became of special relevance in the west of Ireland, an area that was home to the remaining Gaeltacht (Irish-speaking) areas and which were to assume immense significance for cultural nationalists, intent on reviving the Irish language and Gaelic culture throughout the country as a whole. Historically, populist thinking was especially evident in western land policy, where the ideal of basing the rural economy on small-scale farming was carried furthest. It is evident too in manufacturing policy, special measures being introduced in the 1950s to propagate manufacturing in the western 'undeveloped' areas.

Ideological commitment to populism was one thing, the implementation of populist policies proved to be quite another. The ability of relatively larger-scale economic activity and more advantaged areas to benefit disproportionately from populist policies in Ireland has always caused the gap between the theory and the reality of populism to be wide. In addition, a strong move away from populism in certain dimensions of state policy in present-day Ireland, we will argue, is adding significantly to the difficulties being experienced by the small-scale economy and by peripheral areas more generally.

The twelve, designated disadvantaged western counties will provide the special focus of our discussion (see Figure 6.1). Western Ireland, which contains a variety of sub-regions, covers 50 per cent of the Republic's land surface. Only four of the region's 35 towns (at minimum 1,500 people) have a population of 10,000 or more; 75 per cent of its almost 900,000 inhabitants live in rural areas (Brunt, 1988: 109). Alongside measures directed at individuals, households and private sector investors, populist-type attempts have been made in rural Ireland, largely in response to pressure from below, to mobilise whole 'communities' for the development effort. Our discussion will therefore consider not only agriculture and manufacturing but also

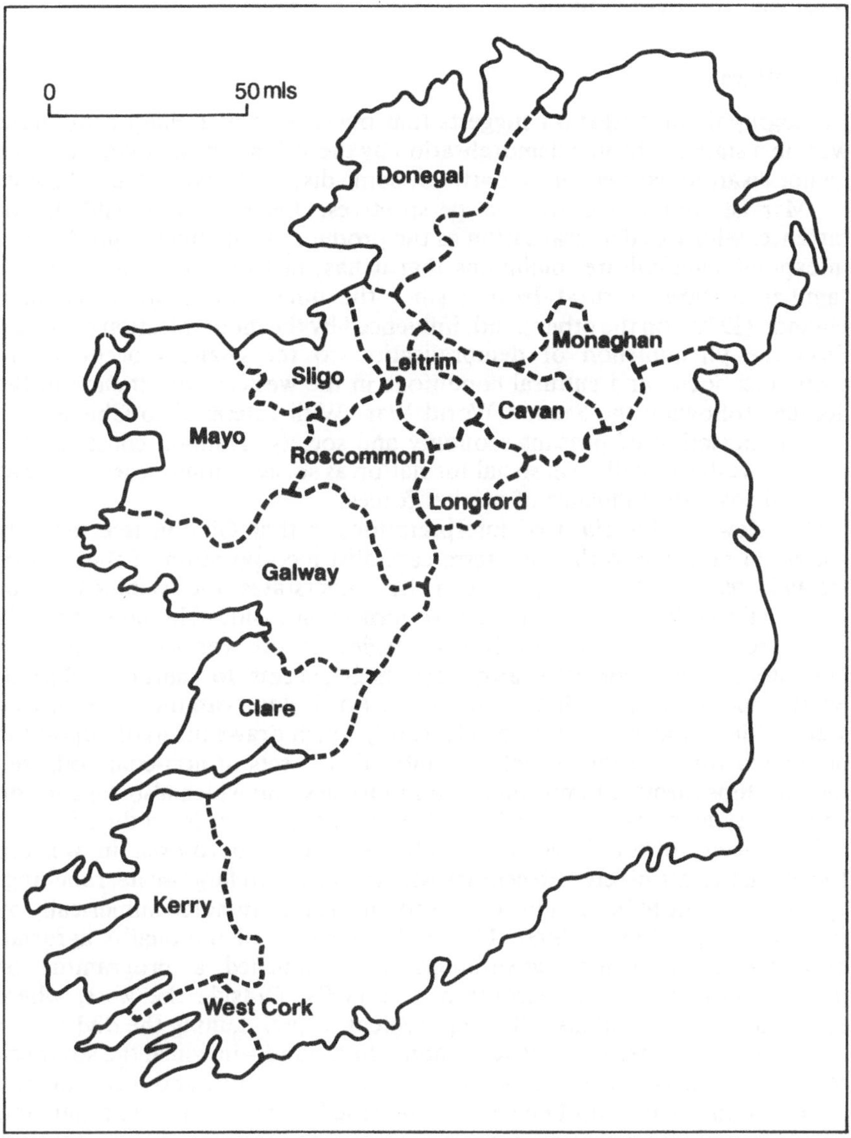

Figure 6.1 The twelve counties of the western region of Ireland

'community enterprise' which, besides being small and located in rural or urban disadvantaged areas, is also notable for the scope it offers for 'participative' development.

Agriculture

Ethnographic investigation suggests that many west of Ireland rural areas were in a state of chronic demoralisation by the 1960s. The aetiology of such demoralisation has become a matter of some dispute between the adherents of Marxist and modernisation perspectives. Peter Gibbon (1973), for instance, who sees demoralisation as the product of expanded reproduction in capitalist agriculture, maintains that it has, in its present form, been a familiar feature of rural Ireland since the nineteenth century. Damian Hannon (1979), on the other hand, influenced by the modernisation position, links the phenomenon of demoralisation to the changes occurring in economic, social and cultural conditions in the western countryside in the decades following the Second World War. With reference to Chayanov's conceptualisation of peasant economy and society, Hannon construes the pre-war western small farm social formation as socially homogeneous and as isolated from the influence of market forces.

Our view of this clash of interpretations is that Gibbon is essentially correct in pointing to the long-term capitalist incorporation of the west of Ireland peasant economy, though he understates the significance of specifically petit capitalism in the western countryside. Hannon correctly points to the successful survival strategies of pre-war western peasant households but incorrectly attributes such success to market isolation. Small-scale primary production in the west of Ireland can more usefully be seen as 'domestic commodity production', which draws primarily upon the household for its labour supply, is embedded in sets of non-commoditised relationships through family and community ties, but which also depends on commodity markets to realise the value of most of what is produced.

Tendencies toward large and small-scale came to co-exist in western Ireland in the late nineteenth century when a pattern of large-scale 'ranching' agriculture came to be established in a countryside dominated numerically by small holdings (Jones, 1983). Under the pressure of nationalist agrarian movements, the British government had launched a programme of redistributionist agrarian reform in the 1890s. Outside the west, where congestion was less intense, the requirement of maintaining the division of labour that comprised the cattle economy in Ireland – in which the southern counties produced calves, the western counties store cattle and sheep and the eastern counties of north Leinster fatten cattle for export – ensured that land redistribution was pursued with much less vigour. Inside the west, the fact that demands far exceeded the supply of redistributable land imposed a formidable constraint. The tendency for what is considered an economically viable holding to increase in size, from about 30 acres in the 1930s to up to 200 acres at present – where cattle farming is concerned (*Farming Independent*, 2 October 1990) – has provided a persisting impediment to radical land reform proposals.

Nonetheless the rhetoric of radical land reform retained its importance into the era of independence, with Fianna Fáil in particular seeking to champion the cause of 'the small man'. The leader of Fianna Fáil, Eamon de Valera, spoke in the early 1930s of dividing half a million acres within five years and settling large number of families on new 30-acre farms. De Valera's populist idyll received its most famous exposition in his 1943 St Patrick's Day broadcast in which he suggested that:

> . . . the Ireland which we dreamed of would be the home of a people who valued material wealth only as a basis of right living, of a people who were satisfied with frugal comfort and devoted their leisure to the things of the spirit; a land whose countryside would be bright with cosy homesteads, whose fields and villages would be joyous with sounds of industry . . . (Browne, 1985: 145–6; Kennedy *et al.*, 1988: 40–41)

More than anywhere the populist ideal as applied to farm size was achieved in the west, where a 64 per cent decrease in the number of over 200-acre farms occurred between 1901 and 1960 in the western province of Connacht, while a 92 per cent increase was recorded in the number of 30–50-acre holdings. Irish farm size trends as a whole, however, suggest that the smallest farms have declined significantly since independence. In 1926, 56.7 per cent of farms were under 30 acres as compared to 24 per cent in 1981; farms of 50–200 acres increased by 10 per cent in the same period. The number of farmers practically halved in Ireland between 1926 and 1981, 'relatives assisting' declined by 90 per cent and paid farm workers by 85 per cent (Breen *et al.*, 1990: 190–1).

Support for family farming has nonetheless been an important objective of Irish public policy. In concrete terms this has meant that full-time family farms have benefited from more favourable tax treatment and that, up to recently, the purchase of farmland by non-nationals has been discouraged. Historically, the Irish state has introduced a number of measures with the explicit aim of improving smallholders' incomes. These include exemption from rates payable on land and the provision of unemployment assistance to smallholders.

In the 1960s, partly in response to local reaction to rural decline, a series of special measures were introduced to improve productivity on small farms, particularly in the disadvantaged areas. Kelleher's (1983) review of the Pilot Areas and the Small Farm (incentive bonus) schemes underlines their technocratic and reformist modernising ideology, yet their reluctance to come to grips with structural issues. Following upon the EC's disadvantaged areas scheme of the mid-1970s, a special EC programme (the so-called Western Package) to combat agricultural disadvantage in the less favoured areas was introduced in 1980. The assessment of a recent commentator, however, is that these measures have 'achieved little in promoting a more viable agriculture' (Brunt, 1988: 77).

Undifferentiated price policy has ensured that the benefits of the Common Agricultural Policy have been regressively consumed. Output and income in Irish agriculture tend to be concentrated in 'the large, specialised dairying, tillage or beef enterprises in the South and East' (Breen *et al.*, 1990: 199). At present, 19.5 per cent of Irish land holders account for 54.9 per cent of cattle numbers while 24.6 per cent of land holders account for 59.9 per cent of dairy cows (Commission of the EC, 1990). As productivity is much higher on the larger farms, these figures underestimate the extent to which output is skewed. Thus the output of the 10,400 smallest milk producers (with 10 cows or fewer) currently amounts to a mere 3 per cent of national milk supply while that of the 6,300 largest suppliers (with 50 cows or more) amounts to 32 per cent (Hurley, 1990). Low-income drystock agriculture tends to be concentrated in the west of Ireland.

Dairying, which offers a better income than dry cattle farming, was encouraged by the state in the non-traditional dairying areas of the west in the 1960s, as were attempts to rationalise milk processing by amalgamating small dairy co-operatives into larger units capable of achieving economies of scale (Curtin and Varley, 1989). The EC's quota/superlevy system of 1984 has had major implications for small milk producers, however. Small dairy farmers with potential for development have found themselves effectively stopped in their tracks. Furthermore, smaller producers have disproportionately availed themselves of the national milk cessation scheme, a pattern that has had serious implications for the viability of the western dairying co-operatives, where small suppliers predominate (Kealy, 1989: 32). The high prices charged, moreover, have resulted in larger, non-western farmers securing the lion's share of what additional quota has been offered for sale (Kealy, 1989: 69).

To alleviate restrictions on the further expansion of production, the Irish state sought in 1987 to channel additional quota to young and small (under 10,000 gallons) producers. The amounts involved, however, have been entirely insufficient[1]. The state, moreover, has shied away from adopting any scheme to redistribute milk quota from the traditional milk-producing south of Ireland to those areas of the west where commercial dairying has been only relatively recently introduced. What has happened is that 'Teagasc', the national agricultural advisory service, has identified the 28,700 milk producers with an average quota size of 15,000 gallons, the single largest supplying category (producing 32 per cent of milk supply), as requiring special attention. Lower service charges apply to these farmers and, in an attempt to overcome the effects of quota restriction, efforts are being made to move them towards farming systems that mix milk production with beef, sheep, suckling or other alternatives (Hurley, 1990).

Paradoxically, much of the populism evident now in Irish agriculture derives from Irish membership of the EC. The official reaction to the crisis of CAP in the 1980s is infused with a populist rhetoric. Commissioner McSharry (1990), for instance, points to the injustice of having 20 per cent of EC farmers consuming 80 per cent of CAP price support, to the threat to the environment posed by intensive, large-scale farming, and to the bankruptcy of a policy that results in massive surplus production.[2] Smallholders, in McSharry's conception, are associated not only with the preservation of the 'social fabric' and a more equitable distribution of land, assets and wealth, but also with a less intensive, more environmentally friendly and custodial agriculture that does not result in costly surpluses. While a multi-stranded or 'integrated' rural development policy and direct income supports are intended to secure the livelihoods of smallholders in less-favoured areas, their survival will depend also on increased market orientation. This, it is officially proposed, can be achieved by farm diversification linked to non-traditional markets and by small farm households gaining a foothold in one or more labour markets.

Manufacturing

The post-partition Free State lacked a strong industrial bourgeoisie. While what large Irish industrialists there were favoured free trade, small-scale industry, on the other hand, favoured tariff protection. In 1923, the Fiscal Inquiry Committee rejected the central proposal of Irish economic nationalism that a protectionist regime for manufacturing be instituted. It suggested, instead, that native industry should take action to counter the negative effects of small-scale production and the high cost of transport and energy (Girvin, 1989).

The republican Fianna Fáil party took office in 1932 and pledged itself to rural industrialisation as part of a programme of import substitutions industralisation. Tariffs came to be used as the most appropriate means of boosting home production and of stimulating small-scale industries (Girvin, 1989: 73). As entrepreneurs were free to make their own locational decisions, the vast bulk of private industry created under Fianna Fáil's protectionist policy came, however, to be concentrated in Ireland's larger cities (Gillmor, 1986: 26). In the 11 western counties, the percentage of the workforce employed in industry increased from a mere 4.8 per cent in 1926 to 7.9 per cent in 1961, as compared to a 13.5 per cent to 23.8 per cent increase in the rest of Ireland (Breathnach, 1985: 177).

When the Undeveloped Areas Act was introduced in 1952 to stimulate manufacturing investment in locationally disadvantaged areas, the incentives provided proved at first incapable of overcoming the many perceived disadvantages of locating in the west. Part of the problem was that the use of special incentives came, as a reult of political pressure from non-designated areas, to be extended to the rest of the country with the Industrial Grants Act 1956 (Girvin, 1989: 180). A prolonged policy debate concerning the respective merits of industrial concentration/dispersion occurred in the 1960s. One of the chief architects of the export-led industralisation programme of the 1960s, T. K. Whittaker, was probably the most prominent proponent of the concentration position. The judgement of the influential *Programme for Economic Expansion* (1958) was that 'with virtually the whole country undeveloped it seems wasteful to subsidise remote area specially by providing more extensive grants'. To concentrate effort in 'the most suitable areas', it was therefore suggested, would 'give better results' (1958: 160).

Concentration, however, proved to be politically unpalatable. The *Second*

Programme of Economic Expansion therefore re-asserted a commitment to dispersion and to achieving 'a more balanced distribution of industry between the different parts of the country' (1964: 163). The use of development centres to forward this end was also approved. Regional policy was discussed in the *Third Programme for Economic and Social Development* (1969) as a means of promoting indigenous industry. The view of the *Third Programme* (1969: 97) was that most small industries 'can operate effectively in relatively small centres thus providing a valuable outlet for rural manpower'. In 1969, the government adopted a dual policy that accepted the merits of both concentration and dispersion. So as to balance the dependence on foreign-led industralisation, a small industries programme had already been launched in 1967 by the Industrial Development Authority (IDA). The financial resources expended on small industry, however, were dwarfed by those absorbed by the new industries programme and used to stimulate large-scale industrialisation. Subsequently, Irish membership of the EC gave a major impetus to industralisation in the west.

The almost doubling of industrial employment (from 12% to 23%), in the designated areas between 1961 and 1983, amounted to about two-thirds of the net national increase in industrial employment. In these years, the designated areas benefited from a 15 per cent differential in their favour in maximum capital grants payable to new industry. Purportedly 'because of their lesser demands', small industries - defined as those employing 50 workers - have been particularly attracted to rural locations (Gillmor, 1986: 28).

Despite this, a prominent feature of the recent wave of western manufacturing is that is has tended to be composed overwhelmingly of large-scale, foreign branch plant projects that have generated very little in the way of spin-off small-scale industrialisation. The employment created typically took the form of female and semi-skilled work (Lucey and Walker *et al.*, 1987: 40, 62). One reason why transnational corporations have tended to source the vast bulk of their raw materials and other inputs abroad was that small western industry in the 1970s was not geared for sub-supply business. And it was not until the 1980s, when a linkage programme was instituted, that local entrepreneurs were encouraged by the IDA to think in terms of seeking sub-supply business in the transnational sector (Smyth and Boylan, 1991). Incoming transnationals, of course, were encouraged by the transfer pricing mechanism to source supplies, components and services abroad and so boost their tax free and repatriable profits (Ruane, 1987).

Recent developments in industrial policy have swung sharply against the peripheral counties of Ireland. The message of the *White Paper on Industrial Policy* (1984) was that resources were increasingly to be devoted to high technology industry and to internationally tradeable sectors.

Priority areas for the IDA, as identified in the White Paper, are those with the greatest growth and job creation prospects, those with the highest unemployment levels and job losses and those with the highest prospective labour force growth. Together with the emphasis now being placed on 'solving national problems and emphasising productivity' (Gillmor, 1986: 32), this shifting of priorities favours the large urban centres of the east and south, seriously affected by deindustrialisation, at the expense of the old policy of regional dispersion. The indications are that many projects hitherto eligible for grant assistance will be excluded from funding in future. As a result of these changes the western counties have effectively lost their designated status (Lynch and Boylan, 1991).

Community enterprise

In the 1980s, the severity of the unemployment crisis forced the state in Ireland to take every job creation proposal seriously. No less than in Britain, a rhetoric of enterprise came to pervade Irish official discourse and, 'communities' were seen, at least in some quarters, as fit subjects to undertake enterprise. In 1989, the Minister for Labour predicted that community enterprise (CE) was capable of delivering as many as 10,000 jobs per year (*Irish Times*, 31 March).[3] 'Community enterprise' has been used in Ireland to refer to local groups attempting to stimulate economic activity either directly, as when they set up in business themselves, or indirectly, when the effort is limited to inducing private or co-operative enterprise to locate in a given locality or workspace.[4] The local groups in question, to use the typology of Esman and Uphoff (1984: 56–68), may assume the form of local development associations, co-operatives, or interest associations.

The number of CE groups grew in Ireland from 50 in 1982 to 250 in 1985 (O'Donnellan, 1985). Our discussion will draw mainly on the experience of *Muintir na Tíre* (People of the Countryside), a national self-help movement with its origins in the Catholic social movement of the 1930s, and on two surveys of CE groups - Breathnach's (1986) study of 16 community development co-operatives in the Gaeltacht (officially designated Irish-speaking) districts and Ó Cinnéide and Keane's (1987) survey of 13 CE groups in the Mid-West region. Three of the most successful Mid-West CE groups, in terms of employment and turnover, have functioned as sub-suppliers for Shannon-based transnational corporations. One of these sub-suppliers will be profiled to provide an insight into managerial strategies and employment relations within this type of CE initiative.

The local development association is perhaps best exemplified in Ireland by the 200 or so community councils affiliated to *Muintir na Tíre*. These endeavour to represent a locality and claim to confer benefits on the whole community. Their special strength has been in organising and lobbying for the provision of local infrastructural facilities (e.g. piped water), improved social services and recreational facilities. While some individual community councils (Killala and Murroe pre-eminently) have been heavily involved in the provision of workspace for small-scale private enterprise, their general weakness in sponsoring CE directly can be attributed to lack of capital, dependence on volunteers, problems of securing community consensus (private enterprise may feel threatened by CE), legal difficulties in holding property and making contracts, as well as to the absence of a comprehensive programme of state support.

With Youth Employment Agency funding, *Muintir na Tíre* head office nonetheless employed an enterprise development officer in 1985, who worked in all with nine would-be CE groups in six counties. Lack of progress, however, caused this animateur to resign in despair in 1987. He has not been replaced and *Muintir na Tíre* head office is no longer active in promoting CE. In light of their experience, *Muintir na Tíre's* national secretary is dubious about the capacity of community councils to sponsor CE directly.[5] He points out that compared to private business, CE groups tend to lack the assets, resources and experience to succeed with what typically are extremely marginal business ideas. Nor can *Muintir na Tíre*, given its own straitened financial circumstances and, with membership morale at a low ebb, hope to compete with specialised state agencies in servicing CE groups. The recent privitisation of the most successful *Muintir na Tíre*-promoted venture, Imokilly Wood Products Co-operative, is seen as further proof of the organisational superiority of private enterprise under capitalism.[6]

The multi-purpose Gaeltacht community development co-operatives (CDCs) have their origins in the Gaeltacht civil rights movement of the 1960s and in the management and administration grant scheme operated by the Department of the Gaeltacht. Rejecting as inadequate the development strategy of the Gaeltacht development agency (previously Gaeltarra Éireann, now Údarás na Gaeltachta), which initially devoted itself to luring manufacturing projects from outside, the approach adopted by the Gaeltacht CDCs has been to stress the desirability of using indigenous natural and cultural resources as well as traditional handcrafts to develop industries based on tourism, fishing, aquaculture etc. To maintain social and economic life in remote areas, the CDCs have also had to involve themselves in providing services; piped water and electricity (on the offshore islands), retail outlets and community facilities are some examples. Cultural activities - music, dancing, drama, Irish language classes - are organised by many of the CDCs.

By the mid 1980s the CDCs had provided small, though locally significant, amounts of employment - 206 full-time jobs relative to a total of 4,000 Gaeltarra Éireann/Údarás na Gaeltachta-assisted jobs. They have additionally improved the income-earning capacities of Gaeltacht households (e.g. by land reclamation), effected cost reductions for smallholders (e.g. in agricultural supplies) and created part-time work opportunities (e.g. accommodating Irish language students).

At the same time, the trajectory of the CDCs has been anything but straightforward. Among the welter of internal constraints against which the CDCs have had to struggle are: local apathy, poor medium-term planning, undercapitalisation and managerial inadequacies. The same tendency for the organisation to become management-dominated as against membership-led, evident in the larger agricultural co-operatives in Ireland, surfaces as well among the small-scale Gaeltacht CDCs, where the appointed manager very frequently ends up deciding policy matters and thus usurping the role of the elected management committee and the shareholders.

Externally, the state's failure to recognise the role of the CDCs in

Gaeltacht preservation and the *ad hoc* and crisis management nature of state assistance has not encouraged CDCs to adopt proper business and financial management procedures. The tension between social and commercial considerations has been a key issue for the Gaeltacht CDCs. Discharging this double burden has not been easy and the surviving CDCs have either tended to abandon service provision for commercial activity or have sold off their business interests to private individuals so as to concentrate on service provision. In these circumstances, state policy can be taken to task for encouraging CDCs to become widely involved yet failing to provide them with adequate capital resources, back-up facilities and education in co-operative methods and procedures. The performance of the Irish state agencies here compares poorly with that of the Scottish Highlands and Islands Development Board which, ironically, based its own scheme on that of the Irish Gaeltacht experience (Breathnach, 1986).

The 13 CE groups found in the Mid-West region are heterogeneous in terms both of their organisational structures (eight co-operatives, three local development associations and two limited companies) and of their activities, which can encompass land reclamation, tourism and the production or provision of a range of 'unsophisticated low value-added goods and services' (Keane and Ó Cinnéide, 1986: 288). Since 'many of the jobs created are marginal in character with respect to rates of wages, holiday pay, and general employment conditions' (Ó Cinnéide and Keane, 1987: 33), CE-based employment in the Mid-West possesses all the hallmarks of a secondary labour market.

Mid-West region CE can avail of the feasibility grants, capital grants for plant and equipment, rent allowances etc., provided under Shannon Free Airport Development Company's (SFADCo) small industries scheme. In recognition of their special needs as *community* enterprise, CE groups can also benefit from special management grants, training and project support. Notwithstanding these and the Gaeltacht special measures, Ó Cinnéide and Keane (1987: 5) suggest that state officials (though SFADCo personnel are judged to be exceptional here) would sooner deal with private rather than community enterprise, viewing the latter as 'weighed down by internal dissensions and external apathy'.

While the cost per job in the Mid-West scheme may be low compared to job creation costs within the IDA's small industries programme, Ó Cinnéide and Keane (1987: 35–8) emphasise that cost-effectiveness measures alone leave out of account many important social benefits and spin-off effects. Private enterprise may even stand to benefit, as when veteran community activists become industrialists in their own right. Nor does SFADCo's initial concern to apply conventional operational criteria – such as job creation targets – conform with Keane and Ó Cinnéide's (1987: 287) view that CE can be soundly established only after a protracted process of community capacity building.

For all that, SFADCo's ultimate insistence on commercial criteria is accepted by these writers as 'desirable' for the reason that is puts 'pressure on each enterprise to show a profit within a reasonable time period' and thus rescues it from dependence on long-term state subvention and 'marginal business status' (1987: 288). However much the ideal of CE may be market driven, the fact remains that practically all CE in Ireland owes its continued existence to state schemes, depending on state financing for temporary enterprise workers, workspace rent subsidies and commercial aid grants.

CEs have been exclusively low technology concerns and as such are unlikely to be in a position to achieve what would be regarded as significant linkages with the dynamic foreign industrial sector. Three of the larger Mid-West CE ventures have nonetheless launched themselves in the sub-supply economy. The attractiveness of sub-supply work to the CE groups concerned lies in the nominal start-up capital costs required, the minimal skill demands made on the local workforce, and the very low running costs (no inventory is involved and state rent subsidies are available).

A brief account is now provided of the management and work practices of the largest of these CE operations, run by a sub-committee of Kilfinane Development Association (KDA) in Co. Limerick, a community co-operative first organised in 1964. This sub-supply business began in 1979 when KDA was controlled by a local priest; subsequently, in 1983, control was transferred to a sub-committee of KDA. In 1989, the business provided on average 20 full-time, 12 part-time jobs and summer work for up to 20 school-leavers. With the exception of the male manager the workforce is almost entirely female. The work consists of manually grading machine-produced electronic components and manually assembling components. Sorters and assemblers are paid on the basis of individual output, though individual assembly jobs are rated differently. An important feature of the business is its seasonality. There tends to be an eight week lull around Christmas during which many full-time workers take a break and live on their social welfare entitlements. Some of these workers are lost to KDA when they leave the area or take up alternative employment.

Although KDA activists see the *circa* IR£100,000 in earning that flows annually as the main benefit of the CE to the locality, the annual wages individual full-time workers earn, ranging from IR£3,000 to IR£5,000, are very low and fall far short of the current average industrial wage in Ireland (IR£7,930.52 for women, IR£12,935 for men). A principle of employee self-management has never been adopted. As KDA views it as 'too important to the village to be allowed out of community control', a proposal to re-organise the business as a workers' co-operative was rejected (Quinn, 1989a).[7] While the workforce is not unionised, it does have two representatives on the nine-member board of management. Worker representatives are recognised to have a legitimate say in recruitment decisions. To judge from the high rate of worker representative turnover, these have evidently found channelling complaints an onerous task.

Over a prolonged period 'business' and 'community' considerations have co-existed uneasily in KDA's day-to-day operations. Community considerations dictate that the different piece-work jobs are rotated so that those on the lowest rated work get a chance to work at higher paid tasks. They also entail a recruitment policy that positively discriminates in favour of those locals most in need of work. In recent years, however, a managerial policy has been adopted that gives business considerations precedence. The balance struck is one in which delivering on time and acceptance of certain quality standards are considered more important than 'equality of opportunity' or the rotation of piece-work.

By and large, CE has not yet established a track record for itself as anything approaching a viable alternative, or indeed as capable of making even a small dent in the jobless figures. Of the 13 CE groups surveyed by Ó Cinnéide and Keane in 1985, five have now ceased to function, either altogether (in four cases) or in the original form (in one case). Only one of the sub-supplier firms survives in its original form. The others collapsed when their customers decided to resume direct responsibility for previously sub-contracted work. In one of these sub-supply businesses, the jobs - based on industrial sewing - were simply lost. In the other, another electronic components assembly operation, five of the workforce were taken on by the transnational corporation and are now 'doing the same work with better wages and conditions'.[8] Meanwhile two of the largest Gaeltacht CDCs have ceased operations, though one of these has subsequently resumed under a different name. No new CDC has appeared since 1977.

Discussion

Are tendencies towards larger scale increasingly in the ascendant in present-day Ireland? The pattern of western industrialisation, heavily dependent on large-scale foreign owned branch plants, provides a fairly clear answer as far as manufacturing is concerned. The indigenous small-scale manufacturing sector has sustained heavy losses and the forecast is that 'the scale effect of the Single Market will worsen (its) competitive position' (Foley, 1990: 242). Large-scale industries, because of their potentially greater employment content, were always favoured by Seán Lemass, the Irish politician most closely identified with state-induced industrialisation since independence (Girvin, 1989). Although the supply of large industries has diminished significantly while existing plants are subject to closure or are prone to labour-saving restructuring, state officials still commonly share the Lemass view. Under the present policy of de-designation and flexible designation, the manufacturing prospects of small-scale industry in the de-designated west have clearly worsened.

The difficulties associated with the transnational sector have nonetheless caused the state to look increasingly to small-scale industry to create sustainable manufacturing-based employment in recent years. Irish industrial policy has set itself the task of creating 20,000 extra jobs per year over the 1989–93 period. A multi-fund operational programme, introduced as part of the reform of the EC structural funds and agreed with the EC Commission in December 1989, is committed to using recruitment incentives, training and management development grants to focus substantial support on small-scale Irish industry.

Some recent initiatives to promote CE have also been launched, or are being assisted, by the Irish state. The Department of Agriculture and Food, for instance, has embarked on a two-year Integrated Rural Development pilot scheme that attempts to involve voluntary groups in the development of their own localities. A programme to create employment by means of 'third sector' companies has commenced in a number of western counties (Mullally, 1989). To bolster its CE programme initiated in 1983, the Youth Employment Agency adopted a CE group development support system in 1987, based on a 'stages of development' approach (Burke, 1989).

In view of the centrality of smallholders and peripheral areas to current EC thinking, the abandonment of populism in agriculture is a more complex matter. The decision to effectively abolish the Irish Land Commission, however, is a clear indicator of the Irish state's willingness to allow market forces rather than state regulation to decide the pattern of land distribution in future. The lack of effective action to remedy the position of smaller milk producers trapped at a low stage of development is another telling indicator. As is the refusal to countenance the transfer of significant quantities of quota to traditionally non-dairying areas in the west. The largely co-operative based milk processing industry is itself edging towards major rationalisation in preparation for the more fiercely competitive post-1992 environment.[9]

Simultaneously, an effort is being made in Brussels to adapt the guarantee fund so as to discriminate positively in favour of small farmers and producers in less-developed areas. The milk co-responsibility levy was thus abolished in less-favoured areas in 1989 and the 1990 farm price package includes measures to extend the EC suckler cow premium to small milk suppliers, to organise a milk buy-up scheme for the benefit of small suppliers in less-favoured areas, and to pay a supplementary ewe premium to sheep farmers. A proposal to extend the disadvantaged areas to cover 72 per cent of Irish farmland looks like it will be approved by the EC Commission.

Given the great attention they have attracted, we must also consider whether the so-called 'alternative enterprises' in rural Ireland – in particular forestry, tourism and aquaculture – are likely to have a populist bias. Generous grants for private forestry – covering 85 per cent of approved costs for landowners and up to 70 per cent for companies, to a maximum of IR£800 per hectare – were provided under the EC Western Package scheme, introduced in 1980 as a means of stabilising the rural population in the western counties. The initial poor uptake by farmers can be seen when the 10-year programme target of 24,000 hectares is compared with the mere 615 hectares that had actually been planted by the close of 1984 (Review Group 1985: 33).

Financial institutions, however, did show an interest and, stimulated by the attractive incentives on offer, began to purchase what was considered locally to be 'good' land and 'large' farms. Such an approach, in the view of the Western Forestry Co-operative (ICOS n.d.: 3), 'militates against rather than improves the atrocious land structural problems in the areas concerned'. By the mid-1980s, investment companies had come to account for more than half the new plantations in some western counties (Kelleher, 1986: 194). Resistance to large-scale private afforestation was co-ordinated in

Co. Leitrim by the Irish Farmers Association whose campaign was guided by the principle that planting should be confined to marginal land.

Although there is some evidence that large farmers tend to dominate agri-tourism in the United Kingdom (Gasson, 1987), eight of twenty east Limerick farmers involved in a state-sponsored agri-tourism scheme have, according to a recent Irish study, holdings of under 50 acres and, of these, seven (five of whom were part-time farmers) were farming fewer than 30 acres (Quinn 1989b: 36). Eight of these agri-tourism farm households have dairying enterprises while eight others have a predominantly dry cattle orientation. Although agri-tourism has not yet become a major income source on 75 per cent of the east Limerick farms, Quinn (1989b: 35) concludes that:

> . . . the smallest farms are more prepared to avail of opportunities to supplement income. The largest farms, who command the most resources, appear to have opted to develop farm enterprises other than agri-tourism.

Small-scale fish farming, 'as an adjunct to small to medium sized agricultural holdings', attracted considerable official attention in the 1950s.[10] Anticipated high profit margins have been critical in the 1980s in constituting salmon farming as an attractive investment opportunity for large-scale capital, intent on pursuing a strategy of diversification. As in Scotland (Ewing, 1987: 11), substantial amounts of Norwegian capital have been invested in Irish finfish aquaculture. Currently the three largest producers - Bradán Mara Teo (owned by Carroll Industries), Fanad Fisheries and Salmara Teo (a subsidiary of the Electricity Supply Board) - account for about 60 per cent of total output. No Irish salmon farm is owned co-operatively.

In comparison with finfish farming, mussel farming gives the appearance of being more accessible to local, small-cale capital as well as more compatible with part-time work patterns and co-operative organisational structures. At present mussel farming in Ireland is concentrated in two major sites - Bantry Bay and north Connemara. Mussel farming, particularly as practised in north Connemara, conforms to the model of domestic commodity production in its small scale, minimal use of wage-labour (though the shellfish co-operative's manager is employed full-time) and the absence of 'expanding cycles of accumulation' (cf. Sinclair, 1985: 15–19).The pattern in Bantry Bay, where mussel production stands at around 1,500 tonnes annually (Herriott, 1987: 35), is not so clearcut. There, local commercial interests have evidently, to a far greater degree than has been the case in north Connemara, seen mussel farmng as an investment outlet (Eipper, 1986: 170–3).

It is possible that the move to larger scale may unleash a process of internal differentiation among members of the co-operative. This may cause the eventual disappearance of domestic commodity production and thus permit it to be seen as a limited, transitory phenomenon. If the shellfish co-operative manages, however, to retain control and individual co-operative members expand in a way that can be handled predominantly by their own and family labour, domestic commodity production may survive and be reconstituted at another, higher level.

Conclusion

While there is then considerable heterogeneity within petit captialism in rural Ireland, the presence of the forces that represent larger scale and spatial concentration is unmistakable. The dominant tendency in development based on natural resources in Ireland is one in which small and large-scale enterprise co-exist but where the underlying trend is toward larger scale. In agriculture, where 20 per cent of Irish farms produced practically two-thirds of output in 1984 (Commins and Higgins, 1987), this trend is clear. Recent changes in industrial policy, moreover, represent a radical departure from the old commitment to spatially dispersed industrialisation. The effects of the new policy regime are likely to impact most on those western areas geographically remote from the handful of large towns. If anything, such effects are likely to be exacerbated with the advent of the Single European Market (Cuddy and Keane, 1990). The trends in alternative industries point the same way. Can we say, on the basis of our discussion, that broad tendencies toward larger-scale economic activity are at work in rural Ireland? And does the evidence support the view that there is a dynamic at work resulting in the position of the peripheral west becoming ever more economically and socially marginalised? Certainly, there is substantial evidence to suggest an affirmative answer to both these questions. At the same time two tendencies – one departing from and the other continuing with the populist tradition that favours small-scale economic activity and peripheral areas – are clearly discernible in Irish policy. The very presence of these tendencies, running in opposite directions, is one powerful barrier to the achievement of any basic measure of 'integration' in state policy.

Originally Irish nationalists were drawn to the ideals of small-scale and dispersed economic activity as a means of stabilising the rural population and as a reaction to the excesses of large-scale urban development, observable in the industrially advanced countries at the end of the nineteenth century. The conditions under which Irish nationalists adopted populism are therefore quite different from those versions of Third World populism espoused only after attempts to implement the mainstream large-scale model of development had failed dismally.

As in other countries, however, the commitment of the independent Irish state to populism has never been more than partial and has not stood the test of time. With economic liberalisation and membership of the EC, tendencies toward larger scale in Irish agricultural and manufacturing activity have been powerfully boosted. The result is that, while opportunities for small-scale manufacturing have undoubtedly been created in the expanding sub-supply economy, much small-scale enterprise on and off the land occupies an increasingly precarious and untenable position. It is against such a background, that low-technology, small-scale 'participative' co-operative and community enterprise in Ireland can be seen to be very much swimming against the tide.

The Irish case illustrates also how the three dimensions of populism we have used to structure our discussion – the preference for small-scale economic activity, the reorganisation of the economy on a decentralised basis, and 'participative' development - provide neither the elements of a coherent ideology nor the basis of an integrated package of policy measures. Perhaps this lack of coherence and integration is best exemplified by the fact that the manufacturing industry dispersed throughout rural Ireland in the 1970s was predominantly large in scale. Moreover, of the three populist dimensions, 'participation' has always occupied a Cinderella status in the eyes of the state. This is more a product of the continuing difficulties small-scale co-operative and community enterprise have experienced in establishing a secure place for themselves within the general framework of a market economy than as a result of the tendency for co-operative and community structures to become management- as against membership-dominated. In its heavy reliance on short-term schemes and programmes that frequently do not extend to the whole population or go beyond the pilot stage, the absence of long-term official commitment is a feature which Irish state policy shares with much Third World state-sponsored 'participative' development.

Notes

1. Almost 13,000 applicants (50 of whom were successful) sought to share in the 250,000 gallons provided as a National Reserve in 1987 (Kealy, 1989: 69).
2. McSharry, in his Galway address, cited the recent outbreak of BSE disease as a more-or-less inevitable outcome of 'unnatural' factory farming.
3. The minister's estimate appears hopelessly utopian in light of the full-time job totals of 84 and 206 recorded respectively by Ó Cinnéide and Keane (1987) and by Breathnach (1986) .
4. Clearly this usage goes beyond the Calouste Gulbenkian Foundation Working Group's (1982: 3–4) suggestion that CE is to be conceived as 'community controlled unlike privately or worker owned' business that is 'distinctive in terms of motivation, objectives and planning and operational needs'.
5. Interview, Tom Fitzgerald, 3 January 1989.
6. A handful of other successful small-scale co-operatives have also opted to go private, a trend also gaining in significance among the large Irish agri-business co-operatives.
7. Lest it be thought that KDA's experience is exceptional, Collins' (1988: 167:72) survey of CE in the Mid-West region provides ample evidence of undemocratic, non-participative work practices.
8. Interview, David Deighan, Community Enterprise Manager, SFADCo, 23 January 1990.
9. The proposal of the Irish Co-operative Organisation Society is that the 50 or so existing co-operatives should amalgamate to form three large groupings capable of surviving in the new business climate.
10. See Erskine Childers to Eamon de Valera, 31 January 1959. State Paper Office, Dublin, S 16384.

References

Bolger, P. (1977) *The Irish Co-operative Movement*. Dublin, Institute of Public Administration.
Breathnach, P. (1985) Rural Industrialisation in the West of Ireland, in Healey, M. J. and Ilbery, B. W. (eds) *Industrialisation of the Countryside*. Norwich, Geo Books.
Breathnach, P. (1986) Structural and Functional Problems of Community Development Co-operatives in the Irish Gaeltacht, in Ó Cearbhaill, D. (ed) *New Approaches to the Development of Marginal Regions: the Organisation and Development of Local Initiative*. Galway, 8th International Seminar on Marginal Regions in association with University College Galway.
Breen, R., Hannon, D.F., Rottman, D.B. and Whelan, C.T. (1990) *Understanding Contemporary Ireland*. Dublin, Gill and Macmillan.
Browne, T. (1985) *Ireland: A Social and Cultural History, 1922–1985*. London, Fontana.
Brunt, B. (1988) *The Republic of Ireland*. London, Paul Chapman.
Bryden, J. (1986) Introduction to Part III: Political and Cultural Aspects of Self Reliant Development, in Bassand, M. *et al.* (eds) *Self Reliant Development in Europe*. Aldershot, Gower.
Burke, S. (1989) Education and Rural Development. A Study of the FÁS Community Enterprise Education Network. Unpublished Master of Rural Development dissertation, University College Galway.
Calouste Gulbenkian Foundation (1982) *Community Business Works*. London, Calouste Gulbenkian Foundation, UK Branch.
Canovan, M. (1981) *Populism*. London, Junction Books.
Collins, T. J. (1988) Community Enterprise: Participation in Local Development. Unpublished Ph.D thesis, St Patrick's College, Maynooth.
Commins, P. and Higgins, J. V. (1987) Towards the Year 2000: Longer-run Trends in Agriculture, in *The Re-structuring of the Agricultural and Rural Economy*. Dublin, An Foras Talúntais.
Commission of the European Communities (1990) *The Agricultural Situation in the Community 1989 Report*. Brussels, Commission of the European Communities.
Cuddy, M. P. and Keane, M. J. (1990) Ireland: a Peripheral Region?, in Foley, A. and Mulreany, M. (eds) *The Single European Market and the Irish Economy*. Dublin, Institute of Public Administration.
Curtin, C. and Varley, T. (1989) Agricultural Co-operatives and Rural Development in the West of Ireland, *Éire-Ireland* 24 (3): 104–19.
Eipper, C. (1986) *The Ruling Trinity. A Community Study of Church, State and Business in Ireland*. Aldershot, Gower.
Esman, M. J. and Uphoff, N. T. (1984) *Local Organizations. Intermediaries in Rural Development*. Ithaca, Cornell University Press.
Ewing, W. (1987) *Report of the Committee on Agriculture, Fisheries and Food on the Development of Aquaculture in the Community*. Luxembourg, European Parliament, Document A2-59/87.

Foley, A. (1990) Indigenous Manufacturing, in Foley, A. and Mulreany, M. (eds) *The Single European Market and the Irish Economy*. Dublin, Institute of Public Administration.

Gasson, R. (1987) Alternative Opportunities for Farmers. Paper presented at Rural Development Conference, Aberdeen, 12 November.

Gasson, R., Crow, G., Errington, A., Hutson, J., Marsden, T. and Winter, D.M. (1988) The Farm as a Family Business: a Review, *Journal of Agricultural Economics* 39: 1–41.

Gibbon, P. (1973) Arensberg and Kimball Revisited, *Economy & Society* 2: 479–98.

Gilbert, A. and Ward, P. (1984) Community Action by the Urban Poor: Democratic Involvement, Community Self-help or a Means of Social Control?, *World Development* 12: 769–82.

Gillmor, D. (1986) Rural Industrialisation, in Breathnach, P. and Cawley, M.E. (eds) *Change and Development in Rural Ireland*. Dublin, Geographical Society of Ireland.

Girvin, B. (1989) *Between Two Worlds. Politics and Economy in Independent Ireland*. Dublin, Gill and Macmillan.

Hannon, D. (1979) *Displacement and Development: Class, Kinship and Social Change in Irish Rural Communities*. Dublin, Economic and Social Research Institute.

Herriott, N. (1987) *Draft Development Plan. Bantry Fish Farming Co-operative Society Ltd*. Unpublished report.

Herriott, N. (1989) Overview of Irish Mariculture. Unpublished lecture delivered to University College Galway Master of Rural Development class group, Leenane, Co. Galway, 7 April.

Holdcroft, L.E. (1982) The Rise and Fall of Community Development in Developing Countries, 1950–1965: a Critical Analysis and Implications, in Jones, G.E. and Rolls, M.J. (eds) *Progress in Rural Extension and Community Development* vol. 1. New York, John Wiley.

Hurley, C. (1990) Increasing Incomes on Farms with Restricted Quotas, *Irish Farmers' Journal* 24 February.

Irish Co-operative Organisation Society (n.d.) Co-operative Forestry Development. Sligo, Irish Co-operative Organisation Society (unpublished paper).

Jones, D.S. (1983) The Cleavage between Graziers and Peasants in the Land Struggle, 1890–1910, in Clarke, S. and Donnelly, Jr., J.S. (eds) *Irish Peasants, Violence & Political Unrest*. Dublin, Gill and Macmillan.

Kealy, E. (1989) A Study of the Structural Changes in Milk Supply 1980–1988. Unpublished Master of Rural Development dissertation, University College Galway.

Keane, M.J. and Ó Cinnéide, M.S. (1986) Promoting Economic Development Amongst Rural Communities, *Journal of Rural Studies* 2: 281–9.

Kelleher, C. (1983) Implications of Different Theoretical Development Perspectives for Policy and Interventions, *Ir. J. Agric. Econ. Rur. Sociol.* 9: 145–60.

Kelleher, C. (1986) Forestry and Farmers, in *The Changing CAP and its Implications*. Dublin, An Foras Talúntais.
Kennedy, K.A., Giblin, T. and McHugh, D. (1988) *The Economic Development of Ireland in the Twentieth Century*. London, Routledge.
Kitching, G. (1982) *Development and Underdevelopment in Historical Perspective*. London, Methuen.
Korten, D.C. (1980) Community Organisation and Rural Development: A Learning Process Approach, *Public Administration Review* 40: 490–511.
Lucey, D.I.F. and Walker, S. *et al.* (1987) *New Jobs in Mayo – A Study of Recent Major Employment Developments*. Castlebar, Mayo County Development Team.
Lynch, C.P. and Boylan, T.A. (1991) The contribution of County Development Teams to rural and regional development, in Varley, T., Boylan, T. and Cuddy, M. (eds) *Rural Crisis: Perspectives on Irish Rural Development*. Galway, Centre for Development Studies, University College Galway.
McSharry, R. (1990) Address delivered at the launch of the Irish Centre for Information and Promotion of Rural Development, University College Galway, 9 June.
Meade, P. (1990) Investing in Forestry, *Irish Farmers' Journal*, 28 July.
Midgley, J. (1986) Community Participation: History, Concepts and Controversies, in Midgley, J. *et al.* (eds) *Community Participation, Social Development and the State*. London, Methuen.
Mullally, P. (1989) A New Model for Rural Development. Paper presented at the Annual General Meeting of County Development Teams, 5/6 October.
Murray, D.J. (1983) The World Bank's perspective on How to Improve Administration, *Public Administration and Development* 3: 291–7.
Murray, F. (1988) The Decentralization of Production – the Decline of the Mass-Collective Worker, in Pahl, R.E. (ed) *On Work*. Oxford, Basil Blackwell.
Ó Cinnéide, M.S. and Keane, M.J. (1987) *Community Self-Help, Economic Initiatives and Development Agency Responses in the Midwest Region of Ireland*. Galway, Social Sciences Research Centre, University College Galway.
O'Connor, E. (1988) *Syndicalism in Ireland 1917–1923*. Cork, Cork University Press.
O'Connor, R. and Whelan, B.J. (1988) *Aquaculture in the Gaeltacht. Its Economic and Social Impact*. Report prepared by the Economic and Social Research Institute for Údarás na Gaeltachta.
O'Donnellan, N. (1985) Community Enterprise: Development Networks, *Focus* 11: 5–6.
The Programme for Economic Expansion (1958). Dublin, Stationery Office.
Quinn, J. (1989a) Profile of a Community Co-operative – Kilfinane Development Association Limited 1964–1989. Paper presented to the Co-operative Development Council Conference, November 24/25.
Quinn, J. (1989b) Agri-tourism and Rural Development. Unpublished Master of Rural Development thesis, University College Galway.

Review Group on Forestry (1985) *Report to Minister for Fisheries and Forestry*. Dublin, The Stationery Office.
Robertson, A.F. (1984) *People and the State. An Anthropology of Planned Development*. Cambridge, Cambridge University Press.
Rondinelli, D.A. (1983) *Development Projects as Policy Experiments: An Adaptive Approach to Development Administration*. New York, Methuen.
Ruane, F. (1987) The Traded Sector: Manufacturing, in O'Hagen, J.W. (ed) *The Economy of Ireland* 5th edn. Dublin, Irish Management Institute.
Sabel, C.F. (1982) *Work and Politics*. Cambridge, Cambridge University Press.
Second Programme for Economic Expansion (1963, 1964). Dublin, Stationery Office.
Sectoral Consultative Committee (1984) *The Development of the Fishing Industry*. Dublin, Sectoral Consultative Committee.
Sinclair, P.J. (1985) *From Traps to Draggers: Domestic Commodity Production in Northwest Newfoundland, 1850–1982*. St John's, Institute of Social and Economic Research, Memorial University of Newfoundland.
Smyth, J.J. (1987) Industrial Development in an Underdeveloped Area: A Case Study of County Mayo. Unpublished Master of Rural Development thesis, University College Galway.
Smyth, J. and Boylan, T. (1991) Industrial Development and the Contribution of Multinational Companies to Local Economic Development: an Irish case study, in Varley, T., Boylan, T. and Cuddy, M. (eds) *Rural Crisis: Perspectives on Irish Rural Development*. Galway, Centre for Development Studies, University College Galway.
Third Programme - Economic and Social Development (1969). Dublin, Stationery Office.
Tovey, H. (1982) Milking the Farmer? Modernisation and Marginalisation in Irish Dairy Farming, in Kelly, M., O'Dowd, L. and Wickham, J. (eds) *Power, Conflict and Inequality*. Dublin, Turoe Press.
Weiss, L. (1988) *Creating Capitalism. The State and Small Business since 1945*. Oxford, Basil Blackwell.
White Paper on Industrial Policy (1984). Dublin, The Stationery Office.
Worsley, P. (1967) *The Third World*. London, Weidenfeld and Nicolson.

CHAPTER 7

The Politics of Rural Enterprise: A British Case Study

Susan Boucher, Andrew Flynn and Philip Lowe

Politics, the state and economic restructuring

Crises of accumulation in capitalist societies necessitate periodic and radical restructuring of production processes to establish new opportunities for profitable investment. One consequence is a reassessment of resources and spaces once considered unproductive or marginal. Not only does this involve economic restructuring and technological change but also politically mediated shifts in social meanings and representations. In Britain since the 1970s, for example, both rural areas and small firms have been given an unprecedented prominence in economic development, even though previously, in their different ways, both were thought of as quintessential backwaters of economic activity (Healey and Ilbery, 1985; Keeble and Weaver, 1986). Indeed, together they have been projected as a specifically rural expression of the 'enterprise culture' promoted by the Conservative Government. At least in terms of promotional images, the traditional rural craftsman vies with the cottage-based telecommuter as a representative agent of the contemporary rural economy; and such dynamic areas of new growth as 'Silicon Glen' (in central Scotland) and the 'Golden Horn' (stretching from East Anglia to south-west England) starkly contrast with the ravaged industrial wastelands of Britain's conurbations. Not only have rural areas come to be seen as presenting a more attractive physical environment than the old industrial towns and cities, but a more amenable social environment too, composed of small-scale enterprises, family businesses and a placid labour force, little marred by sharp social conflicts or the 'dependency' culture (National Economic Development Office, 1989; ACRE, 1990).

A number of factors have contributed to this reassessment. The prominence given specifically to small firms in industrial policy has various tributaries. For some time, 'new right' politicians and supply-side economists, amongst others, have diagnosed fundamental weaknesses in the British economy arising from labour market rigidities rooted in industrial corporatism, the entrenched position of the big unions and Britain's relatively concentrated industrial structure. With the sharp up-turn in business closures, bankruptcies and lay-offs during the recession of the late 1970s and early 1980s, the formation of new firms came to be seen more immediately as a key to economic renewal. The promotion of small businesses and self-employment was a means not only to counteract mass unemployment but also to nurture economic independence and initiative. At the same time, small 'venture' companies in certain sectors were recognised as potential agents of innovation and entrepreneurship (Storey, 1982; O'Farrell, 1986). Last but not least, small, family-run firms have a special place in the Tory pantheon as expressions of personal independence, thrift and enterprise.

The emphasis on rural areas as zones of economic potential has a separate provenance though there is clearly an affinity between small firm and rural development ideologies. This is rooted in the distinctive nature of rural labour markets, characterised by local conjunctions of working class quiescence, petit-bourgeois ownership of capital and small-scale enterprises (Bradley, 1984). In addition, statistical evidence, particularly from the 1981 census, of counter-urbanisation and an urban–rural shift in manufacturing employment, has suggested an economic and demographic buoyancy in many rural areas that is absent from much of urban–industrial Britain (Champion, 1983). New firm formation rates, for example, have been shown to be higher in rural than in urban areas (Gudgin and Fothergill, 1984). At the same time, some of the new wave technologies, particularly bio-technology and information technology, are seen to favour rural locations. As Howard Newby has put it, 'for the first time since the industrial revolution, technological change is allowing rural areas to compete on an equal basis with towns and cities for employment' (*Financial Times*, 8 December 1989). Certain political factors have also played a part. On the one hand the Government, anxious to curb agricultural supports and surpluses, has devised various programmes to encourage farmers to diversify their businesses. On the other hand, with the curtailment of gross depopulation, a disparate rural lobby has sought new justifications for rural development programmes, based on arguments to do with the inequalities and opportunities rural areas present, rather than their marginality or backwardness. There has been a consequent shift in rural regional policies from state-led industrialisation programmes and inducements for inward investment to the promotion of indigenous small firms and self-help initiatives (Pettigrew, 1987; Day *et al.*, 1989; Cloke, 1990).

Part of the Thatcherite rhetoric of the enterprise culture is about getting government off the back of business, of rolling back the state, of freeing-up markets. However, the effecting of such profound changes necessitates a very active and interventionist role for the state. Not surprisingly, therefore, government's involvement in economic restructuring is surrounded by contradictions, not least where it must mediate highly contested shifts in social meanings and representations, as in the field of rural economic development. But academic analysis of economic restructuring has largely failed to acknowledge this central, if ambivalent, role.

The literature on restructuring does imply that different relationships will emerge both locally and functionally between the state, capital, labour and other political interests (Massey, 1984; Duncan and Goodwin, 1988). In conceptualising this fragmented state in political terms the work of Rhodes (1986, 1988) is helpful. He has drawn attention to the differentiation of government into policy networks each comprising a nexus of interest groups and professional associations dependent upon one another for resources of one sort or another. Being largely dependent on outside bodies including local government to implement policies, it makes sense for central government, seeking to contain within manageable bounds its range of consultations, to aggregate them where possible, and it is from the interaction between the interests involved that distinct policy networks emerge (Rhodes, 1986).

The state is thus not to be conceptualised as a whole, as serving the interests of a particular class, or the long-term interests of capital (Rhodes, 1986). Equally, it would be mistaken to regard government as an arbiter of the public interest. Rather, what Rhodes argues, is that, while central government can and does act to maintain existing socio-economic structures, it has a whole set of responsibilities, including regulation, legitimation and allocation, where it interacts with particular policy communities. These policy communities have their own interests, as well as a regard for their own self-perpetuation and power, just as do the central departments of government; and the question of what these interests specifically are is to be determined by empirical research rather than theoretical fiat.

To take further our understanding of the state and politics and their relationship to economic restructuring now calls for empirical evidence, and we present here our analysis of the role of various agencies in the field of rural economic development and specifically rural small firms policy. After reviewing the stances of central government departments and relevant national agencies, we focus on a particular county, Devon, so as to illuminate the role of local authorities and other state agencies at the local level. The fragmented structure of institutional approaches to rural economic development can itself be seen as the outcome of competing interpretations of rural needs (Wright, 1984); and, by forcing a reordering of policy networks, the social redefinition of the countryside that is accompanying economic restructuring is bringing these contradictory interpretations into sharper relief.

Central government approaches to rural economic development in the 1980s

As in so many other policy spheres, there has been a marked shift in the approach of central government to rural development in the 1980s. Neo-liberal ideas have been brought to bear, though certain specific factors have mediated their influence in this field. First, the countryside remains the heartland of the Conservative Party and therefore rural policy has been more receptive to traditional shire Tory interests. Second, agricultural over-production has demanded pragmatic responses within a supranational (i.e. European Community) policy framework which is fundamentally welfarist, Keynesian and interventionist. Third, the government has become increasingly sensitive to a rising tide of popular concern for the environment. A final issue remains, not specific to the rural field, and that is what the real impact of Ministers' neo-liberal radicalism has been in practice, after being filtered through the devolved structures of British administrative government.

Several distinct, though overlapping perspectives have emerged on rural development in general and rural economic diversification in particular within central government, reflecting separate departmental priorities. The Department of the Environment has pursued the objectives of liberalising the planning system and promoting a more pro-development and market-oriented outlook with local planning authorities, while also being sensitive to rural conservation and amenity concerns. The Ministry of Agriculture, Fisheries and Food (MAFF), anxious to reduce food surpluses and the cost of agricultural support, has sought to encourage the diversification specifically of farm businesses, not least by establishing a more favourable context for re-use of agricultural land and redundant farm buildings.

The Department of Trade and Industry (DTI), unsympathetic to both the supply-side constraints posed by the planning system and traditional approaches to regional policy, and spearheading the Government's drive to foster an 'enterprise culture', has pressed for rural areas to be opened up to new types of investment and development. Regional policy has been revised in order to 'encourage the development of indigenous potential within the Assisted Areas with the long-term objective of self-generating growth in these areas' (Cmnd. 9111, 1983). However, the territorial ministries responsible for the administration of much regional policy - the Scottish Office, the Welsh Office and the Northern Ireland Office - have tended to take a somewhat more pragmatic, dirigiste and corporatist approach to rural and regional development than the DTI (Moore and Booth, 1989).

In general, the Government has sought to leave to the judgement of the private sector questions to do with the demand for and appropriate location of industrial and commercial development. In keeping with this stance, it has pressed local authorities to accept that a much wider range of economic activities are suited to rural locations. The government's main planning Circular for England and Wales, *Development Control - Policy and Practice* (22/80) urged that when 'small scale commercial and industrial activities are proposed especially in existing buildings, in areas which are primarily residential or rural, permission should be granted unless there are specific and convincing objections such as intrusion into the countryside'. The introduction of new jobs into rural areas, it was argued, would 'prevent loss of services and keep a viable and balanced community'. The circular did stress, however, that 'the Government's concern for positive attitudes and efficiency in development control does not mean that their commitment to conservation is in any way weakened'.

Circular 16/84 on *Industrial Development* stressed the need for new enterprises in the countryside and commented that 'many small-scale buildings can be fitted into rural areas' without causing unacceptable disturbance. The desirability of converting redundant buildings was reiterated, and planning authorities concerned about intrusion into the countryside were reminded that many light industrial uses are less noisy than some agricultural activities. Authorities were also urged to be more flexible and responsive to employment-generating proposals and not to be hamstrung by restrictive policies in development plans.

Circular 2/86 specifically addressed the needs of development by small businesses. In an apparent contradiction of Circular 22/80, local authorities were exhorted not to reject proposals 'merely because planning policies restrict development in the countryside. The main object of such policies must be to protect the landscape from unacceptable new buildings, and they should not be used to prevent new uses or development whose impact on local amenity and infrastructure would be marginal'. This seemed an attempt to modify significantly rural restraint policies and to limit them to questions of design and landscaping.

Most local authorities do seem to have responded to pressure to allow more employment uses into the countryside. Government commissioned research on rural employment concluded that the planning system had 'not represented a severe constraint on the development of small businesses' (JURUE, 1982, p 59). The exceptions were activities thought to be too intrusive or out-of-keeping such as car repairing, scrapyards and haulage contracting.

The relaxation of planning policies, however, has tended not to favour the development of agricultural land but rather the re-use of existing buildings, including surplus farm buildings, large country houses and redundant institutional complexes (such as mental hospitals). The landscape may thus be little affected as new uses are accommodated in established structures. Indeed, the justification for such conversions is often put in terms of the need to preserve traditional buildings. Not only does this help to placate rural amenity concerns but it also reinforces the comfortable myth of an unchanging countryside. Central to this myth is a social aesthetic, long promoted by a paternalistic rural lobby which elides physical beauty and social fitness. A locality which looks right must also, it is assumed, support a desirable way of life. The 'attractive' conversion of traditional buildings to 'suitable' crafts thus combines moral, aesthetic and utilitarian values which conversely are offended by the transformation of barns and other farm buildings into up-market residences for outsiders (Watkins and Winter, 1988).

Responsibility for the actual encouragement of small firms is shared between a number of government departments and agencies. The White

Paper, *Releasing Enterprise* (CM 512, 1988) argued that wealth creation should be facilitated through the simplification of the mass of rules relating to business, but particularly those which affected small firms and start-ups, and by encouraging such firms to seek professional advice.

A strong emphasis on small and medium-sized businesses has figured prominently in the DTIs Enterprise Initiative which the Department itself has characterised as marking a significant break from previous industrial policy. A deliberate effort has been made to relinquish the Department's traditional sponsorship of industrial sectors in favour of an approach oriented to the freeing-up of markets and the improvements of business competitiveness and efficiency. A key element in this strategy has been the provision of a range of consultancy services to enhance the management skills of small and medium-sized businesses. The Department has accordingly sought to work closely with and through local business organisations, such as Chambers of Commerce and local Enterprise Agencies, rather than the national trade associations typically dominated by large companies, that formerly were its main partners (Cm 278, 1988).

The Department of Employment has gone even further in this regard by turning over funds and responsibility for training and economic development to a network of Training and Enterprise Councils each under the control of local businessmen (LSE, 1990). Through its Small Firms Service, this Department also provides advice and support to establish small businesses, and counselling, to tackle basic business problems.

More specific measures for rural economic development have depended on particular agencies. The main regional agency for rural England is the Rural Development Commission (RDC), which comes under the auspices of the Department of the Environment. Unlike its sister agencies in mid-Wales and the Scottish Highlands and Islands, the RDC was in the past much less involved in general economic planning and programmes of state-led industrialisation and infrastructural improvements. Its principal role, instead, has been to develop small factories and workshops (Clarkson, 1980; Minay, 1990).

The RDC's concern with small enterprises (defined as those with fewer than 20 skilled workers and under 100 workers in total) long predates central government interest in the 'small firms solution' to macro-economic problems. The approach, partly inspired by the philanthropic and visionary efforts of Leonard Elmhirst (for a long time a member of the Commission) to revive the Dartington estate and the surrounding mid-Devon economy, has its roots in the established conception of the Commission's role as being about 'mopping up' the worst excesses of a long process of agricultural restructuring, as well as in the rural social aesthetic mentioned above with its portrayal of craft activities in small workshops as the most appropriate form of rural industrialisation (Young 1982). The emphasis on small businesses also represents a broadly laissez-faire approach to economic development in rural England which has resonated well with Thatcherite precepts.

The RDC has found it difficult, however, to cast off the traditional craft image. Even so, with the need for all such agencies to address the high levels of unemployment that Britain has experienced throughout the 1980s, it has sought to shift its attention away from the very smallest firms (i.e. those with five or fewer employees) and it has edged cautiously into supporting certain types of service industry, as well as manufacturing. In addition to sites and premises, the RDC now provides a wide range of business services including advice, training and credit. In 1984, in keeping with a general move to much greater selectivity in regional aid it also began to target its support more; Rural Development Areas were designated on the basis of the problems of rural unemployment, depopulation or service decline which they suffered. For each area the RDC, in collaboration with the local authorities and other agencies, draws up a Rural Development Programme, covering both social and economic development and this guides the RDC's provision of financial assistance.

One of the distinctive features of British rural development policies and agencies is that traditionally they have existed in isolation from agricultural policy-making. The opportunity to pursue social objectives or non-agricultural products through the farm support mechanisms has until recently been eschewed by MAFF in pursuit of a narrow notion of what constituted productive agricultural activity. Such provisions as those in the EC's Less Favoured Areas Directive (75/268) for grant-aiding tourism and craft enterprises were simply ignored by the UK government. Belatedly, though, there has been a marked change in outlook. The 1986 Agriculture Act broadened the responsibilities of MAFF to include the 'economic and social interests of rural areas'. The following year MAFF launched its farm diversification scheme as part of a package of measures (the so-called ALURE package, which emanated from the interdepartmental working group on Alternative Land Use and the Rural Economy), which also included a weakening in MAFF's vetting powers over development involving agricultural land, and the farm woodland scheme.

The diversification scheme, which is administered by MAFF's Agricultural Development and Advisory Service (ADAS), is to encourage farmers to get involved in activities such as adding value to products, recreation and tourism, and on-farm marketing. A number of types of enterprise are eligible, including: processing of farm produce; craft manufacture; agricultural machinery repair; farm shops; holiday accommodation; catering; sports and recreation facilities; livery; and educational facilities relating to farming and the countryside. 'Heavy industry, or light industry not normally expected in a farm environment' is excluded, as are certain forms of recreational sports including hunting, motorsports, shooting and war games. The level of grant – 25 per cent (or 31 per cent for farmers under 40 years of age) on investments up to £35,000 – has been pitched to appeal to the small or medium-sized farmer (and contrasts with a ceiling of £74,000 in relation to other MAFF grants). The take-up has been fairly low, amounting to just over one per cent of all significant farm holdings after two and a half years of the scheme. Farmers have been most responsive in the South West, with 2 per cent of Devon farmers getting involved. Accommodation and recreation (including horses) have proved the most popular activities, with the former preponderant in the traditional tourist areas, and the latter in urban fringe areas, especially in the South East (see Figure 7.1). Partly because of the activities taken up and because of the limited involvement in the scheme, it is likely to have only a marginal impact, if any, on surplus agricultural production.

Figure 7.1 Distribution of Approved Capital Grants under the Farm Diversification Grant Scheme by enterprise type, for England, January 1988–May 1990

Enterprise	n	(Percent)
Accommodation and Catering	772	(43.59)
Recreation/Education	306	(17.28)
Processing of Farm Produce	211	(11.91)
Horse-based	199	(11.24)
Direct Marketing	186	(10.50)
Letting of Enterprise	66	(3.73)
Craft Manufacture	20	(1.13)
Agricultural Machinery Repair	11	(0.62)
Total	1771	(100.00)

Economic development policies in Devon

Turning to our case study county of Devon, we now examine how the economic development and planning policies of the county and district councils interact with different economic interests to produce changing definitions of rural Devon (see Figure 7.2).

The county lies in the south west of England, a region lacking a major industrial conurbation and, at 41 per cent, having the highest proportion of its manufacturing jobs in rural areas of any British region (Fothergill *et al.*, 1985). Over the past 30 years the region has tended to experience above-average growth levels particularly in the service sector (see Figure 7.3). Of course, such trends will not be uniform in their impact and Devon's position is such that it does not possess the extreme economic peripherality of its Cornish neighbour, but is not dominated by a major metropolitan economy. If a process of economic restructuring is occurring here, then it is taking place in a county which, despite its rural image, has a long history of involvement in extractive industries, tourism and small-scale industrial activity. The degree of self employment exceeds the national average, accounting for one in five of the workforce in 1981. Employment in companies with fewer than 200 workers is also significantly above the regional and national average. During the 1980s the Devon economy, in keeping with the region as a whole, became very buoyant; unemployment fell to just below the national average in a county which has traditionally suffered well-above-average unemployment rates. Most of the new jobs were in service industries. But wage rates remained considerably below regional and national levels.

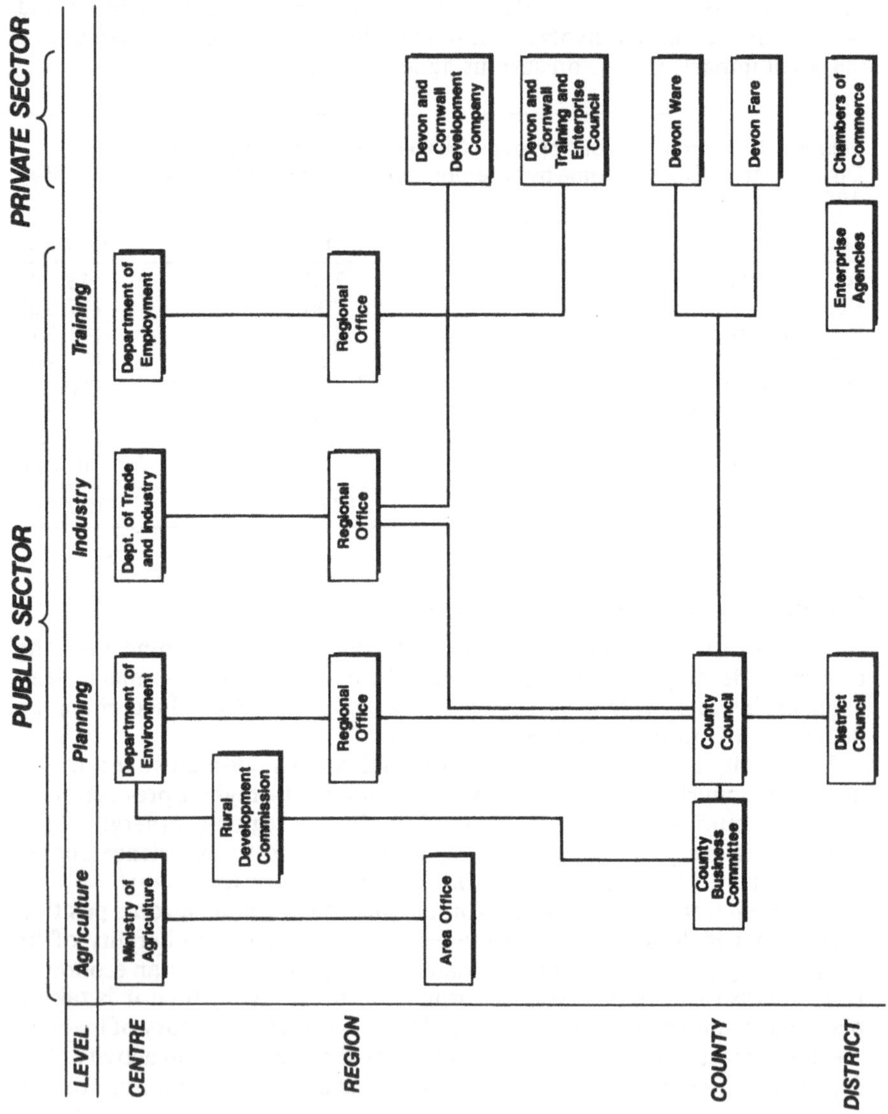

Figure 7.2 Structure of organisations promoting economic development in rural Devon

Source: adapted from Wright, S. (1982)

Figure 7.3 Sectoral distribution of employment in Devon, by percentage of persons employed, 1951 and 1981

	Percent	
Sector	1951	1981
Agriculture, Forestry & Fishing	22.71	5.33
Mining & Quarrying	1.55	0.80
Energy & Water	1.39	1.62
Manufacturing	12.88	17.77
Construction	8.37	7.50
Distribution	12.41	15.36
Communications & Transport	6.03	5.03
Insurance, Banking & Finance	1.36	2.86
Other Services	33.31	43.74
	(100)	(100)

Source:
1951: General Register Office, Census 1951, Industry tables (100 per cent)
1981: OPCS Census 1981 Economic Activity Tables (10 per cent sample)

In the past, the county and district authorities in Devon have pursued somewhat different approaches to intervention in economic development but now seem to possess a common logic. This is the pursuance of policies encouraging growth, orientated primarily if not exclusively towards the satisfaction of expressed local employment and business needs. To understand how this position has come about, it is useful to consider briefly the post-war evolution of the county's economic planning.

The post of Industrial Development Officer for the county was created in 1958, with the stated intention of publicising Devon to outside manufacturers. As well as marking a growing awareness of the emergence of a pool of surplus labour particularly outside the largest towns, the appointment also coincided with the creation of the post of Chief Planning Officer, and was thus part of a more general movement to professionalise the county council's administrative structure, and to reinforce its strategic role in the development of Devon. The planning context at this time was one in which the county was seen as remaining too heavily dependent on its traditional staples of agriculture and tourism, and with encouragement seen to be needed to expand light manufacturing in the principal towns. During the 1960s most of the county was accorded assisted area status in recognition of its persistently high unemployment levels. This provided a context in which the county council could expand its own role in promoting Devon to outside interests, and it became a major provider of employment land. The redefinition of assisted areas in 1984, in an effort by central government to make regional aid more selective and cost effective, excluded the bulk of Devon except for part of the west of the county and the Plymouth Travel to Work Area. The county council was left, alongside Plymouth City Council, as the main agent promoting industrial development in the county.

Over the years the effort to attract manufacturing employment has met with moderate success though the main area of employment growth has been in the service sector. At the same time, Devon has remained a favoured destination for retired people and for other, geographically mobile, social groups, attracted not least by its 'unspoilt' villages, towns, countryside and coast. In a relatively low-wage area, the steady influx of more mobile and usually more affluent people has stirred up resentments and tensions. A recurrent theme of local politics across the county is the 'invasion' by non-local people and capitals. The development boom of the 1980s fuelled such reactions, and additionally provoked middle-class amenity opposition to the growing pressures on the Devon countryside.

Such anti-growth sentiments came to a head in the county council elections of May 1989, when rural and small town Conservatives ousted an urban-based Alliance administration. The new council rejected a consultation document issued by their predecessors, entitled 'Devon in 2001' which was to have been the basis for the Third Alteration to the Structure Plan. The document was written on the assumption that the county would become increasingly popular for inmigration towards the end of the century, and that the main issue at stake was where that growth should be accommodated. The new council reconstructed the debate into fundamentals of whether growth should be encouraged or resisted. In the words of Ted Pinney, the leader of the council, 'we don't want Devon exploited by *outside speculators*... but to provide a planning document which allows young people to stay and work in their own area' (Western Morning News 10 May 1989, emphasis added). Pinney is also the leader of East Devon District Council, which personifies the view that any new development allowed outside the major settlements should be oriented towards the satisfaction of locally expressed needs.

Such an outlook has been repudiated by the county council's Director of Property who for a number of years has been responsible for its economic development activities. He has publicly attacked the 'powerful vested interests' in the county behind maintaining a low-wage economy, and has argued that:

> We have to change all that, and go for excellence – nothing less. We need to encourage the employer, *local or incomer*, who puts a premium on investment in training and equipment. Only in that way will we bring local productivity and hence earnings up, to enable our young people to bid for homes in competition with retired bankers and businessmen (Andrew Smy, *Western Morning News* 5 July 1990, emphasis added).

Such arguments are behind the view that 'The County has successfully promoted itself out of disadvantage but the economy of Devon continues to need the Council's special attention' (DCC, 1989, p28). Nevertheless, it is evident that the county council's proactive strategy for economic development faces a significant political threat. That strategy has incorporated several elements besides the provision of serviced employment land. With Cornwall County Council, for example, Devon supports an overseas promotional bureau (the Devon and Cornwall Development Bureau) which encourages inward investment particularly from the USA and Japan by companies seeking a European base to penetrate the European Community market. The emphasis in the promotional literature is on low wages and non-unionisation; in short, green labour in a green environment. The Bureau, however, has sought to attract companies which pay wages above the county average and which provide training programmes for their workforces.

Another key element in the county council's economic development strategy is the promotion of rural development. Approximately 70 per cent of Devon is designated a Rural Development Area wherein, with the support of the Rural Development Commission, the county and district councils jointly pursue a rolling programme to provide employment land and workshops and improve community facilities and services (see Figure 7.4).

Devon is Britain's leading dairying county, and concern over the potential impact of milk quotas, imposed in 1984, prompted the county council to examine alternative means to support farm incomes and diversify the rural economy. The favoured solution was that of added value to primary products and the Devon Fare and Devon Ware initiatives were launched to try to establish a greater market profile and identity for the county's traditional food and craft industries under a promotional banner espousing 'quality from the countryside'. These are not merely marketing ploys but reveal something of the way in which the county council would like to see rural Devon develop. Thus Devon Fare and Devon Ware, which have corporate status, along with the Devon Farm Holiday Group, are part of a wider strategy looking to market 'countryside culture' as a complete package to a discerning clientele, with the overall aim being to establish a 'viable "cottage industry" to integrate with the county's existing economic base' (DCC, 1987).

With the exception of the farm holiday scheme, however, the nature of the companies involved bears little relation to the imagery on which the strategy relies. The individualistic character of small crafts producers has meant that it is difficult to integrate them into a collective organisation. Similarly, the involvement of most farmers in the processing of food is minimal; the participants have often been branches of nationally-based processing companies. The more ambitious plans, moreover, to set up a Rural Commodity Exchange as a marketing co-operative for novel livestock and crop products, to establish a Devon production policy, and to create Rural Enterprise Centres combing craft, tourism and retailing activities 'epitomising Devon life' (DCC, 1987, p12) have not materialised.

Echoes of the last of these, however, can be found in the county's rural tourism strategy. Once again the equation of 'quality' with 'rural' is pursued in an approach designed to appeal to the well-to-do 'empty nesters' and not to the 'bucket and spade brigade' (Interview with Rural Development Officer, DCC, 22 June, 1989). The image portrayed is one of 'rural heritage and culture' and there is thus potential for conflict with the traditional,

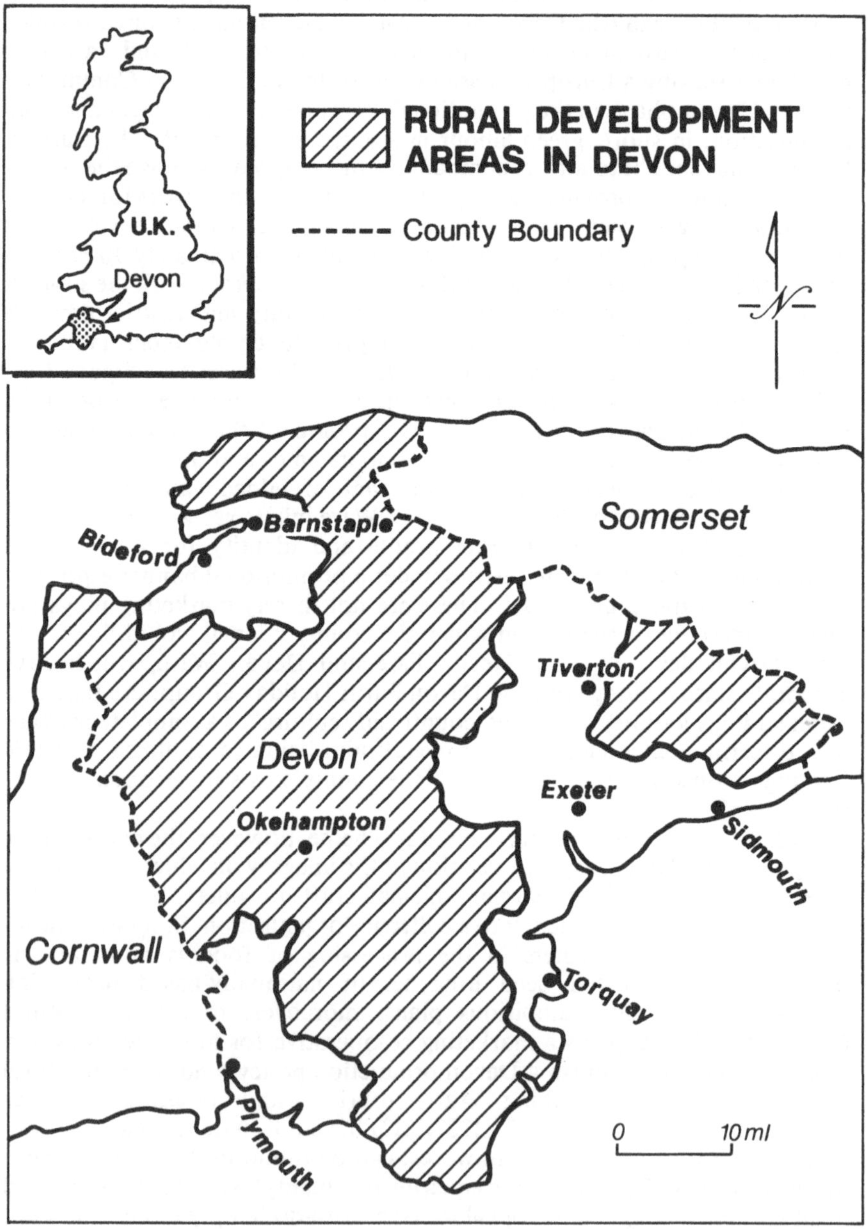

Figure 7.4 Devon and its Rural Development Areas

seaside tourist industries of Torbay and North Devon whose fortunes have stagnated in recent years. The hotelier and tourist interests that are strong in Torbay are not well represented on the county council and the outlook from the rest of the county is of the need to constrain any further development of mass tourism.

The recent switch in the political control of the county council spells the demise of some of its more interventionist approaches to economic development, particularly those which tended to be more at the service of external capitals. For example, it is unlikely to maintain past levels of investment in employment land which over the years have yielded more than 220ha of serviced land. With pressures for the council to dispose of what land and premises are still in its ownership, one officer interviewed commented that 'we're working ourselves out of a job' (Interview with Industrial Development Officer, DCC, 4 September 1989). With rising land values and an expanding industrial land market, it is hoped that private developers will step in, though council officials have warned that this is 'a service which the private sector is reluctant to support owing to the length of time it takes to get a return on investment' (DCC, 1990, p 19). The draft Third Alteration to the Structure Plan, issued in 1990, seems to concede this point in confirming policies to furnish 'serviced employment sites' and 'small workplace units in the rural settlements to meet local needs', but specifying in both cases that priority be given to 'areas not provided for by the private sector'.

Crucially, also, the Rural Development Programme enjoys strong support from the district councils. In the past the many small local authorities which existed before local government reorganisation usually took a very parochial view of external development. Market towns such as Honiton and Okehampton, with little industry but dominated politically and economically by small traders and professional people, were often keen on expansion and attracting outside investment of any kind (Martin, 1965; Glyn-Jones, 1983). In contrast, towns with a traditional manufacturing base (such as Barnstaple and Tiverton) tended to be more restrictive in their outlook, and more protective towards established companies (Grant, 1977; Glyn-Jones, 1983). With the creation in 1974 of consolidated district councils, each encompassing several towns and many villages, the politics of local economic development became more complex, but an ideology of localism (rooted in a tradition of Independent politics which largely survived reorganisation) still prevails, with most of the districts keen to respond to local employment needs but also concerned to safeguard the interests of local firms and businesses.

Teignbridge District, lying in the Exeter-Torbay hinterland, was the first of the seven rural districts in Devon to create a specialist Industrial Liaison Section, in 1981, which was set up following a loss of 400 jobs from the closure of a local firm. All but two of the other districts followed suit, creating specialist industrial or economic development posts in response to the high levels of unemployment of the early and mid-1980s, prompted also by the setting up of the Rural Development Programme. In contrast to the traditional stance of the county council, the districts seem to have a positive but unwritten policy to favour local firms. In the words of the Teignbridge Industrial Liaison Officer, 'we're very committed to local firms . . . they're the ones who've been with us when things have been bad' (Interview with Industrial Liaison Officer, Teignbridge District Council, 7 September 1989). Such attitudes are reflected not only in the districts' own programmes of industrial promotion and support but also in the ways in which they use (or refrain from using) their forward planning and development control functions to allocate land to employment uses. Such land allocations tend to favour local firms and their specific expansion needs. Proposals to convert redundant farm buildings have also usually been well received.

Following the change in the political control of the county council in 1989, such a localistic orientation seems set to determine the approach to economic development of the county also. The willingness of small town and rural Conservatives to intervene in the market to safeguard local interests is out of step with the 'new right' element that has been dominant in the leadership of their own party since the accession of Margaret Thatcher. Increasingly, this is a source of tension not only within the Conservative Party nationally but also in right-wing business and political circles within Devon.

In particular, there has recently emerged a pro-development private sector consortium called the Devon and Cornwall Development Company (DCDC) which has some of the largest firms in the region as Founder and/or Board members, including English China Clays (ECC), Mowlems, the Royal Docks at Devonport, the Duchy of Cornwall, Blue Circle, Peter de Savary and the banks. A key figure was ECC's corporate development manager who is also a regional councillor for the Confederation of British Industry. The firms involved all have strong interests in developing the two counties and they have provided four-fifths of the Company's initial five-year funding.

With its specific regional orientation and the patronage of the Department of Trade and Industry, the company represents a new style of 'regional policy', the key features of which are moves towards the privatisation of policy, with the private sector expected to take over the responsibility for much of policy delivery (an example of what Streek and Schmitter (1985) refer to as 'private interest government'), and a shift in the emphasis from financial assistance to selected firms to the creation of a climate more favourable to business growth and competitiveness.

The Company's efforts to boost economic development in the region include seeking to stimulate the supply of employment land, lobbying central government for investment in transport infrastructure, promoting skilled training, organising business information networks and helping mount export drives. Working groups in agriculture and fisheries have also been established to overcome what the Company feel to be the excessive fragmentation within these industries which prevents effective marketing and development of their products.

The activities of DCDC have aroused much scepticism, if not hostility, in local government circles. Its strongly pro-development stance runs counter to the policies of some of the local planning authorities. The Company's

Managing Director, who is a former economic and executive director of the Confederation of British Industry, is quick to make a distinction between protection and preservation of the countryside and disparages those who would put the county 'in aspic' (Interview with Managing Director, DCDC, 16 August 1989). A pleasant rural environment is, however, seen as an essential element in an 'identity package' which the Company wishes to promote in order to attract firms whose highly skilled workforce value a 'quality' landscape in which to live and work.

With its more direct links with central government, the Company is seen as trying to circumvent the local authorities. In one district, for example, there is resentment that it carried out a survey of commercial land availability without consulting the local authority even though it approached tenants of industrial units owned by the authority (Interview with Economic Development Officer, South Hams District Council, 6 April, 1990). The assessment of a senior officer of the county council is that DCDC has failed to appreciate 'how difficult it is to do things here against the tide' (Interview with Industrial Development Officer, DCC, 4 September 1989). In consequence, though the Company's brochure refers to sites in the region ripe for commercial development, it has found it exceptionally difficult to assemble a portfolio of land to offer prospective industrialists (Interview with DTI South West, 26 February 1990).

It is evident that DCDC operates in a separate and competing policy network to that of the local authorities. The local government officers responsible for economic development at county and district levels, and those involved in the preparation of the Rural Development Programme (frequently the same individuals) meet and exchange information on a regular basis, amongst themselves and with the Rural Development Commission. There is also a two counties' forum of economic and industrial development officers which has had some acrimonious meetings with the Company. The Company is not part of this network, although there are indications that it is eager to acquire some of the functions presently carried out in the public sector. Already it is responsible for the allocation of government grants to the county's enterprise agencies, it has set up its own Rural Enterprise Loan Fund and it oversaw the creation of the Devon and Cornwall Training and Enterprise Council. Moves have also been made to incorporate the two county councils' DTI-supported promotional organisation (the Devon and Cornwall Development Bureau), and the Company's Managing Director has expressed interest in taking over some of the present functions of the Rural Development Commission.

Conclusions

Whereas for years the RDC (whose history goes back to 1909) and the other rural development agencies existed as forgotten outposts of regional and rural policy, now they find themselves in a crowded policy field facing competition from other agencies. In the case of a farm tourism enterprise, for example, the interested farmer could conceivably seek assistance from the Regional Tourist Board, ADAS, the RDC, the Sports Council or the Small Firms Service of the Department of Employment (Slee, 1990).

The various agencies, though, embody different conceptions of rural needs – conceptions whose very relevance is being challenged by rural restructuring. MAFF, for instance, interprets rural diversification as farm diversification and conceives of this narrowly as on-farm, ancillary enterprises; whereas the RDC sees it as building workshops, arranging advice and loans for small businesses and providing community facilities in villages and country towns. In this sense both reflect their history as well as their clientele. But inevitably, the latter are changing.

Traditionally, for example, the RDC has been strongly oriented to the needs and interests of rural businesses, and the voice and experience of local business people were specifically incorporated into its credit and advisory services through Small Industries Committees in each county (now County Business Committees) Increasingly, though, loans come from the commercial banks to which the Commission introduces customers and with which it operates schemes for preferential rates and top-up loans. The task of financial assessment, previously the responsibility of the Small Industries Committees, is now undertaken jointly by the banks and the RDC's Business Service staff. The gatekeeper role of local capital has therefore, to a considerable extent and with some irony, been replaced by that of finance capital.

Rural restructuring and diversification spell even more profound changes for the traditional clientelistic relationship between agriculture departments and the farming community. As Slee (1990) explains:

> Diversification to most agricultural support agencies remains one adjustment strategy which may be occasionally recommended as a tack-on enterprise to the mainstream agricultural activity. From the agency point of view agriculture must retain its uniqueness for this uniqueness is the underlying rationale for the agency's existence. But, as the traditional agricultural constituency declines in numbers, a policy of institutional apartheid, separating out farmers from other rural entrepreneurs, becomes increasingly untenable.

This helps explain the resistance amongst agricultural agencies towards diversification and integrated rural development programmes, and their lack of interest in the promotion of off-farm employment opportunities compared with on-farm diversification. Inevitably, though, the blurring of traditional distinctions between economic sectors that diversification necessarily entails does challenge the integrity of those agencies based on such distinctions.

Since the 1970s, local authorities have assumed a more active role in the formulation and implementation of policies for rural economic development, especially since their establishment of economic development officer posts. Urry (1990), however, adduces the following reasons why this group is unlikely to emerge as the core of a professional policy community dominating policy making in this field:

> First, local economic development is the province of several different individuals and agencies in a local authority and hence it is difficult to form them into a cohesive group that is able to pursue a professionalisation strategy of occupational closure. Although there is a putative organisation of local economic development officers, they cannot present themselves as having a particularly distinct set of technical skills and competencies. Secondly, this is reinforced by the fact that in a period of limited new economic activity they are in straightforward competition with each other in order to attract the few footloose plants and offices available. Furthermore, economic development is a local authority activity about which most councillors will believe themselves to be well-informed. They will thus be unlikely to allow it to be treated as a purely technical matter. [Finally] there have been considerable challenges to the professionalisation of well-entrenched groups from both central government and from the lay public. This has meant that those occupations concerned with economic development, which had yet to professionalise, will almost certainly not now be able to do so.

Urry concludes from this analysis that 'Localism rather than professionalism will thus be dominant in British local economic policy' (p 191).

The lack of a strong professionalised policy community leaves space for other interests to emerge as competing policy actors – interests attracted by the broadening opportunities rural areas present. The Devon and Cornwall Development Company provides an interesting example, formed to spearhead a pro-growth lobby for the far South West.

Previously, within Devon, there had been no formal, county-wide groupings to put forward the views of industry, other than the Devon Stone Federation. There is, for example, no county federation of chambers of commerce. The existing business associations represent highly localised commercial and manufacturing interests, reflecting the county's largely fragmented and small-scale industrial structure (Baker, 1990). DCDC, however, represents other fractions of capital – namely the major mining, construction and financial interests in the region. The antagonism that it has provoked amongst some of the local chambers of commerce suggests that it is unlikely to be able to establish its particular pro-growth strategy as a hegemonic project. This contrasts with the experience of certain other regions, most notably Scotland, with a more coherent industrial structure and a stronger regional identity (Moore and Booth, 1989).

Moreover, as a species of 'private interest government' sponsored by the DTI as part of its Enterprise Initiative and within the Government's overall imperative to 'roll back the state', DCDC illustrates some of the contradictions inherent in state action in pursuit of free enterprise. Inevitably, it has found itself at odds with the local authorities, most of whom favour more selective and locally oriented policies of economic development and resent the encroachment of a private lobby into areas which they regard as legitimately their responsibility.

One of the major contributions of the restructuring literature is to direct attention towards localities, and from a political perspective this means sub-central government, especially local authorities and regional agencies, and the interests which surround them. Studies of local politics thus have an important contribution to make as it is here that policies formulated and services delivered within separate networks are refracted. It is because this process of implementation takes place within defined administrative boundaries that insights can be gained into the linkages and discontinuities between networks and organisations.

Nevertheless, exploring the differences amongst local political systems and their links to the centre can be extremely complex. Essentially the problem is to establish the scope for independent action of local authorities and regional agencies, or perhaps more accurately, the perceptions within an authority of its ability to adopt a particular strategy. The challenge is to move beyond a discussion of location-specific factors which favour or hinder action, and to investigate the networks and links with fractions of capital as these affect the prospects for economic development.

The way in which the rural is represented can have crucial implications for the perceptions of the type of development to be encouraged. Not surprisingly, district councils have a more parochial and paternalistic attitude towards development, whilst the Devon and Cornwall Development Company, with its alternative links to large-scale capital and government, is keen to encourage regional growth and development by external capitals. The promotion of different types of investment is related to notions of a desired countryside. For DCDC the image is of a pleasant rural setting that needs to have its economic profile raised by encouraging high-technology industries with high added value. Meanwhile, the districts are more concerned to promote an image of rural Devon which remains rooted in agriculture and small-scale businesses which employ the skills of local labour. In the struggle between these organisations as well as farmers and amenity groups, the image of Devon is being continuously redefined.

References

ACRE (1990) *Country Work*. Cirencester, ACRE.

Baker, J. (1990) Initiative test for the West's chambers, *Western Morning News* (6 August): 4.

Bradley, T. (1984) Segmentation in local labour markets, in Bradley, T. and Lowe, P. (eds) *Locality and Rurality: Economy and Society in Rural Regions*. Norwich, Geobooks.

Champion, A. (1983) Population Trends in the 1970s, in Goddard, J. and Champion, A. (eds) *Urban and Regional Transformation of Britain*. London, Methuen.

Clarkson, S. (1980) *Jobs in the Countryside: Some Aspects of the Work of the Rural Industries Bureau and COSIRA 1910–1979*. Wye College, Department of Environmental Studies.

Cloke, P. (1990) Community development and political leadership in rural Britain, *Sociologia Ruralis*, 25: 305–22.

Cm 9111 (1983) *Regional Industrial Development*. London, HMSO.

Cm 278 (1988) *DTI – the Department for Enterprise*. London, HMSO.

Cm 512 (1988) *Releasing Enterprise*. London, HMSO.

Day, G., Rees, G. and Murdoch, J. (1989) Social change, rural localities and the state: the restructuring of rural Wales, *Journal of Rural Studies 5*: 227–44.

Devon County Council (1987) *Rural Devon: Adapting to Change*. Exeter, DCC.

Devon County Council (1989) *Devon County Council Property Department Stewardship Report*. Exeter, DCC.

Devon County Council (1990) *Employment in Devon: Policies and Programmes 1989*. Exeter, DCC.

Duncan, S. and Goodwin, M. (1988) *The Local State and Uneven Development*. Cambridge, Polity Press.

Fothergill, S. *et al.* (1985) Rural industrialisation: trends and causes, in Healey, M. and Ilbery, B. (eds) *The Industrialisation of the Countryside*. Norwich, Geobooks.

Glyn-Jones, A. (1983) *Planning in action: vision and reality in a country town*. Exeter, Devon County Council.

Grant, W. (1977) *Independent Local Politics*. Farnborough, Saxon House.

Gudgin, G. and Fothergill, S. (1984) Geographical variation in the rate of formation of new manufacturing firms, *Regional Studies 18*: 189–220.

Healey, M. and Ilbery, B. (eds) (1985) *The Industrialisation of the Countryside*. Norwich, Geobooks.

Keeble, D. and Weaver, E. (eds) (1986) *New Firms and Regional Development in the European Community*. London, Croom Helm.

JURUE (1982) *The Planning Problems of Small Firms in Rural Areas*. Birmingham, Joint Unit for Research in the Urban Environment, University of Aston.

LSE (1990) *TECs: Early Experiences*. London, London School of Economics.

Martin, E. W. (1965) *The Shearers and the Shorn: A Study of Life in a Devon Community*. London, Routledge and Kegan Paul.

Massey, D. (1984) *Spatial Divisions of Labour: Social Structures and the Geography of Production*. London, Macmillan Education.

Minay, C. (1990) The Development Commission and English Rural Development, in Buller, H. and Wright, S. (eds) *Rural Development: Problems and Policies*. Aldershot, Avebury.

Moore, C. and Booth, S. (1989) *Managing Competition: Meso-Corporation, Pluralism and the Negotiated Order in Scotland*. Oxford, Clarendon Press.

National Economic Development Office (1989) *Work in the Countryside*. London, NEDO.

O'Farrell, P. N. (1986) *Entrepreneurship and Industrial Change*. Dublin, IMI.

Pettigrew, P. (1987) A bias for action: industrial development in Mid-Wales, in Cloke, P. (ed) *Rural Planning: Policy into Action*. London, Harper and Row.

Rhodes, R. A. W. (1986) *The National World of Local Government*. London, George Allen and Unwin.

Rhodes, R. A. W. (1988) *Beyond Westminster and Whitehall: the subcentral governments of Britain*. London, Unwin Hyman.

Slee, R. W. (1990) Agency Roles and the Development of Farm Diversification in the UK. Paper presented to the Congress of the European Society for Rural Sociology, Giessen, July.

Storey, D. J. (1982) *Entrepreneurship and the New Firm*. London, Croom Helm.

Streek, W. and Schmitter, P. C. (eds) (1985) *Private Interest Government: Beyond Market and State*. London, Sage.

Urry, J. (1990) Conclusion: place and policies, in Harloe, M., Pickvance, C. G. and Urry, J. (eds) *Place, Policy and Politics: Do Localities Matter?* London, Unwin Hyman.

Watkins, C. and Winter, M. (1988) *Superb Conversions?: Farm diversification: the farm building experience*. Centre for Rural Studies, Royal Agricultural College Cirencester/CPRE.

Wright, S. (1982) *Parish to Whitehall: Administrative Structure and Perceptions of Community in Rural Areas*. Gloucestershire Papers in *Local and Rural Planning 16*. GLOSCAT, Department of Town and Country Planning.

Wright, S. (1984) Pigeon-holed policies: agriculture, employment and industrial development in a Lincolnshire case study, *Sociologia Ruralis 24*: 242–60.

Young, M. (1982) *The Elmhirsts of Dartington – the Creation of a Utopian Community*. London, Routledge and Kegan Paul.

Index